MY MOODY MEMOIRS

By Paul Nevin
2005

xulon PRESS

Dedicated to the 10,000 students who have graced my classrooms

CONTENTS

CHAPTER 1
EARLY IMPRESSIONS OF MOODY BIBLE INSTITUTE

A. First Impressions of Moody

I remember it well. In early May 1963, I took the second airplane flight of my life. I was born in Southern California, where I lived for 29 years, and this was my first-ever visit to Chicago. The occasion? To be interviewed and trial-teach for a possible faculty position in Bible and theology at the Moody Bible Institute. In those days there were turtleback busses (the rear of the bus was shaped like a turtle's back) that ran from O'Hare Airport to down-town Chicago, so I climbed aboard at O'Hare. The combination of heat and humidity was so great that I felt faint for lack of oxygen. I rolled down the window and stuck my head out to get more air! I wondered if I could possibly survive in Chicago!

I met Dr. Alfred Martin, the current dean of faculty, whose office was on the third floor of Fitzwater Hall. I was impressed that he was a "charming and godly man," as I recorded in my diary. He interviewed me in an informal setting, the old Sweet Shop on Institute Place. I was also interviewed by S. Maxwell Coder, dean of education, and by John Bass, manager of personnel. I thought it amusing that Mr. Bass discussed retirement benefits with me before I was hired!

Dr. Martin gave me a detailed tour of the Institute's buildings, which then consisted of two city blocks clustered snugly together between La Salle Street and Wells Street on the Near North side of Chicago. A feeling of spaciousness was created by a paved road called Institute Place that divided the campus into two parts, with sidewalks and benches on either side. There were no trees, grass, flowers, or shrubs—only concrete, bricks, and asphalt. (Someone put a few concrete planters with flowers in them on the property, and the students jokingly called the planters their campus!) Today the campus contains approximately ten blocks from Chicago Avenue to Oak Street north to south, and from La Salle Boulevard to Franklin Street, east to west, (and even west of Franklin Street with the soccer field and Walton Street buildings), with lots of beautiful landscaping.

I was deeply moved by the missionary and Practical Christian Work (later known as Practical Christian Ministries) prayer meetings that were going on around the school as I toured. I was also struck by the quality and neatness of the buildings and grounds. The three auditoriums, of which Torrey-Gray was the largest, seemed ample and were well kept.

The far-reaching work of the Moody Bible Institute around the world, which Dr. Martin described, inspired me. I was delighted with "the spiritual caliber, earnest demeanor, and joyous adjustment of the students." [Personal Diary, May 8, 1963]. I was told that ten per cent of all Protestant foreign missionaries had received training at MBI. The radio broadcasting facilities amazed me. (Moody Bible Institute was a pioneer in Christian radio broadcasting.) Moody also pioneered in missionary aviation. This entailed flight and aircraft mechanics training for young men (and an occasional young woman) who became missionary bush pilots. The Aviation Department was begun and capably managed by Paul Robinson. It was originally in Elmhurst, and then relocated to the Wood Dale Airport, near O'Hare. It later moved to Elizabethton, Tennessee. Today, the aviation program functions in conjunction with a community college in Spokane, Washington. Over the years, Moody's flight program has trained about half of the world's missionary pilots. The Audio-Visual Department, then managed by Wayne Buchanan, was on the cutting edge at the time, and has maintained excellence through the years since as the Media Center, today known as The Education Technology Services Department.

Moody Institute of Science, founded by Irwin Moon and based in Whittier, California, produced Christian films that made compelling arguments for a Creator-God who lovingly and brilliantly provided for all of his creatures, especially human beings. These films were shown in high schools, military bases, churches, and foreign countries wherever they were requested, and led to many conversions to the Christian faith. Moody Institute of Science also put on live science demonstrations. In later years I saw some of these and made sure our children also got to see them. An earthquake heavily damaged the headquarters of Moody Institute of Science in Whittier in 1987, and the operation was moved to Chicago. Eventually, MIS stopped producing films, and switched to videos so that both small groups and large could view them more conveniently. This part of Moody was renamed Moody Video. Moody Literature Mission (later renamed Moody Literature Ministries) gave away millions of Christian books and booklets to evangelical missionaries who distributed them around the world. Moody Correspondence School has been very influential in providing in-depth Bible study opportunities to Christians all over the globe. Thousands of pastors, missionaries, and laypeople have been taught in God's Word through the correspondence courses. Even thousands of prisoners have been instructed in Scripture while incarcerated.

As an insatiable bookworm, I was also thrilled with Moody's library, which at that time contained about 65,000 volumes and occupied two floors of Crowell Hall. (Today, it has much greater space in the lower level of the Sweeting Center, and has grown to some 209,000 volumes/items. This includes some 156,000 actual books in the main part of the library.)

I had a long talk with Dr. Martin that first evening, during which we got to know each other better. The next day, Dr. Martin took me to meet President Culbertson. Though a very dignified man, he was surprisingly informal and invited us to remove our suit jackets, since he was in his shirtsleeves. He talked mostly about Moody's doctrinal distinctives, which I already admired and with which I fully agreed. Moody is not only fully orthodox in doctrine and interdenominational, but also evangelical and premillennial. Its evangelistic and missionary passion was also one of the factors that attracted me to Moody. Dr. Culbertson showed us souvenirs from Africa that missionary alumni had sent him. It was obvious to me that missionary ministry was close to Dr. Culbertson's heart.

B. God Prepared Me for Moody

I was not a total stranger to the Moody Bible Institute before I applied for a position there. One of the first books I can remember my Christian mother reading to me as a small boy was *The Life of D. L. Moody,* by his son, William R. Moody. The book is still in my library—its spine taped and its pages browned with age. This book imparted to my young imagination a love and admiration for the great evangelist from Chicago, and the Bible Institute he had founded. But in my wildest dreams I never thought that I would have the privilege some day of teaching there. One of the things that deeply moved me about Mr. Moody was that he was a very ordinary person whom God chose to use to the utmost. I felt I was a very ordinary person also, and I wanted God to use me as well. My mother also read to me several books from the Moody Colportage series, and later I had read some of these on my own. A title from that series that still sticks in my mind is *Lost in London.*

Another early contact with Moody Bible Institute was through a field man employed by Moody's Stewardship Department. While I was in high school (perhaps 1949 or 1950), he came to our house by my mother's invitation and showed a 30-minute film on school life at MBI, and left me the current academic catalog. That made a deep impression on me, and I thought it would be great if I could become a student there.

A third encounter with Moody came when I saw a "Sermons from Science" demonstration at a Youth For Christ rally in Pomona, California. Irwin Moon presented it. Later, I viewed several different films produced by the Moody Institute of Science at churches and Youth For Christ rallies. While I was a student at Pacific Bible College of Azusa, California, I had shown some of these myself when I sponsored and led a Bible club on my former high school campus.

Finally, as a Bible College student I had read a number of books published by Moody Press, and had received good information and inspiration from them. In particular, I recall *The Epistle to the Romans*, by James Stifler.

When I applied for a teaching position at Moody, I was living alone in a one-room bungalow in Hermosa Beach, California. In the late summer of 1962, I was hired by Culter Academy as a part-time teacher and bus driver. Starting in Redondo Beach, I drove a school bus 25 miles through all-city traffic to Culter Academy in Los Angeles, picking up students along the way. Then I taught eleventh graders American history and journalism (neither of which I was well prepared for), and repeated the route back to Redondo Beach in the afternoon. I wrote letters of employment inquiry to five different Bible colleges and seminaries, asking if they needed teachers in Bible or theology. Two did not reply, two others said no, and Dr. Martin at Moody replied yes, they would like to explore the possibility with me. I had never heard of a resume, but I did state my testimony to Christian conversion and my educational and Christian service background.

As I stated in my letter of application, I had received my B.A. in Biblical Literature from Pacific Bible College of Azusa (now Azusa Pacific University). I obtained my B.D. (Bachelor of Divinity) and Th.M. (Master of Theology) degrees from Talbot Theological Seminary (now Talbot School of Theology). Further, I had completed all class work for the Th.D. (Doctor of Theology) degree at Dallas Theological Seminary, and successfully finished seven two-hour written exams for the doctorate. I still needed to complete my lengthy dissertation (which eventually grew to over 500 pages!) and take my oral exam. I received good references from Dr. John Walvoord, then president of Dallas Theological Seminary, and from Dr. J. Vernon Mc Gee, pastor of the great Church of the Open Door, in downtown Los Angeles, where I was a member for ten years.

I had engaged in a wide variety of Christian ministries since 1950. These included a neighborhood Bible club, Sunday school teaching in various churches, and teaching in a variety of youth and adult groups at the Church of the Open Door. I was also invited to preach in numerous churches in Southern California.

I was on several teams that preached at the Los Angeles County Jail. It was an eerie feeling to go through several huge iron gates, each of which was locked behind us. The guard in charge would yell out, "Church on the line!" The prisoners who wanted to participate would move to the front gate of their cellblock. Though it took a great deal of courage (converts were often harassed by fellow prisoners), many prisoners made decisions for Christ when the simple message of God's love in Christ was presented. Sometimes we preached the gospel to the "hot tank." This was where murderers were housed. When convicted, some of them would be transferred to death row. I remember one prisoner whose bunk was near the front cellblock gate. He was lying on his bunk, pretending to read the paper. But on closer inspection, I noticed that his newspaper was upside down! He was actually listening to the message, but didn't want other prisoners to know it!

I had a special opportunity to teach Sunday school in the Los Angeles County Juvenile Hall, a facility for youth who had committed all kinds of serious offenses. I also had the wonderful privilege of teaching the Church of the Open Door's largest adult Sunday school class—the Maranatha Class, where 200 to 300 attended. I have vivid memories of teaching 1 Corinthians in that class just before I came to Chicago. I had a great time of it until I came to 1 Corinthians 7, about marriage, divorce, and the single life. I was still single at the time, but I did manage to get through the chapter before departing for Chicago. I never finished the rest of the book, but my successor picked up where I left off and completed 1 Corinthians.

I was a chaplain intern at the John Wesley Los Angeles County Hospital for a year (1957-58), where I visited many patients and shared the gospel with them. I was reminded of the uncertainty of life when some of "my patients" passed away.

For three semesters (1962-63) I taught in the newly formed Los Angeles Bible Training School, located in the Watts district of Los Angeles. The Church of the Open Door, where I was a member, sponsored the school. At first there were only two faculty members, and both of us served without pay. I helped formulate the curriculum for the entire school. I loved my students, and they loved me. All of my students were African Americans, and their ages ranged from the 20's to the 60's. Most had spouses and children, and they were employed in the Los Angeles area and active in their churches. I taught a course in the Gospel of John, the history of missions, and one in the Epistle to the Romans. The Romans course doubled for a course in homiletics (how to prepare and deliver sermons), since many of the students were already pastors. When I gave them my own outlines of various paragraphs in Romans, they took these outlines and preached on them in their churches the following Sunday!

I wrote and taught a church membership course for junior and junior high kids at the Church of the Open Door. For a short time I was assistant pastor at the Bible Brethren Church in the Lincoln Heights district of Los Angeles.

All of these opportunities gave me a chance to check out my spiritual gifts, and I concluded that my primary gift was teaching. I loved to teach more than anything else, especially Bible and theology, and I got consistently positive feedback whenever I taught.

It was also to my advantage that, as I learned later, Dr. Martin preferred to hire teachers who had a doctorate from Dallas Theological Seminary, his alma mater. He felt (and I think rightly so) that Dallas graduates would be true to the Word of God and good models of a Christian lifestyle to their students at Moody. In 1963, about half of the Moody faculty members were Dallas grads. Moody and Dallas Seminary have had a continuing mutually beneficial relationship over the years.

How did God prepare me to teach at the Moody Bible Institute? In ways beyond my comprehension! These included not only my experience in Christian service, but also my difficult family background. My father was crippled at 10 when he fell out of a tree. Because he had running ulcers from his injuries, he was never very well. He disdained to go to college, thinking himself smarter than his teachers. He went from job to job, most of them lasting less than a year. Part of the problem was, he was so independent-minded and stubborn that he had trouble getting along with his bosses. Eventually he developed tuberculosis of the spine, and died in surgery at the age of 42.

My mother was born with a cleft palate, and the resulting shame at hearing her own voice, plus being emotionally rejected by her mother and her sisters, made her a bitter woman. She married my father because she felt that, since both were handicapped, they were equals. She did have a high regard for education, and went through college with high grades. She even began a master's degree in education. That was cut short by a severe illness. The marriage produced five sons, of whom I was the youngest. I was four years old when my father died, leaving my mother and us five boys, ages 4 to 16, in poverty. (I was born in 1932 in Pomona, California, near the beginning of the Great Depression.) My mother became a widow with five unruly boys to rear, with no means of support but an occasional small gift from her parents, who lived in Mc Pherson, Kansas. They paid the rent for our house (at first, $10.00 a month, and eventually, $20.00 a month). About the only jobs available to women at that time were nursing, secretarial work, and teaching. She had taught elementary school briefly before she married, but there was no way she could consider working when she was responsible for five young sons!

Just before my birth, my mother became very ill with a large tumor. She thought she would surely die. An elderly, godly man came and shared the gospel with her. Although my mother had attended church all her life, she did not understand the necessity of trusting Christ as Savior and Lord. When this elderly stranger shared the gospel with her, she placed her faith in Christ and was miraculously healed of her tumor at the same moment. For a time, she became a joyful, grateful woman who gave her testimony to all who would listen. She yearned for my father to come to Christ as well. But after a few years, the bitterness about her cleft palate and rejection crept back into her life. Her bitterness poisoned our entire family.

My oldest brother, Jack, who was a skilled metal smith, developed Alzheimer's disease before his death at 75. The next brother, Robert ("Bob") became mentally ill as a teenager. He suffered from schizophrenia, manic depression, and paranoia. He was in and out of California mental hospitals all his life, beginning at age 16. He died at 51 when, as a pedestrian, he was hit by a car. My third brother, George, is 80 at this writing, and is probably more healthy and "normal" than any of the rest of us. He was a civil engineer. The fourth brother, Francis ("Frank") was a geo-physicist who explored for oil and gold and did soil testing. He was an adventurer, living dangerously all his life and dying at 69 of cirrhosis of the liver, a result of alcoholism. Why did God choose me and not them, to serve him in this way? Perhaps I will never know.

After my father's death, our family was on welfare for a time in the County of Los Angeles. Somehow we always had enough to eat, though it wasn't necessarily the food we wanted! Jack and Robert worked to help support the family. Our clothes were almost always second-hand, and there was no money for toys or luxuries. Two of my older brothers, George and Frank, did manage to graduate from college. George went to the University of Southern California while in the U. S. Navy, and so his tuition was paid. Frank went to Antioch College in Ohio, where he studied engineering alternated by a work program. This enabled him to put into practice what he had studied and also to pay for his tuition. After serving in the U. S. Army during World War II, he was able to complete college at the University of California, Los Angeles, on the G. I. Bill of Rights.

By the time I was old enough for college, the tuition money was available, since my mother's parents had died and left her a sizable inheritance. There was enough to pay for my college tuition, and tuition to two theological seminaries. Despite many problems, the Lord abundantly provided for me to get a good education!

As a youth, I learned to get along with very limited financial resources. Because I grew up during the Great Depression, I developed a frugal mindset. This made an indelible stamp on my personality that remains to this day. When I applied to Moody, I didn't even think to ask what the salary would be. I was so excited about the prospect of teaching the Bible that I didn't care much about salary. After all, I was still single, and I needed only a modest remuneration to survive and even thrive! (My first year's salary turned out to be $5,000 a year, before taxes.)

I shall always be grateful that my mother led me to faith in Jesus Christ when I was about five years old. I attended church regularly, but we moved from church to church frequently, and this hampered my spiritual growth. However, it also taught me about different denominations and doctrinal perspectives, and that knowledge helped prepare me for my teaching career at Moody, which is inter-denominational. As a boy and as a young man, I listened to many different Christian radio broadcasts in Southern California, and this, too, taught me that God has his faithful children in many different churches. When I was in Bible College, I majored in Bible and minored in missions. The Lord gave me a real interest in missionary work, and for a time I considered becoming a missionary. Gradually I decided that I was not suited for a cross-cultural missionary career, but I have never lost my interest in missions. My concern for the world missionary enterprise has led me to encourage my students to become involved in missions as well.

On the second day of my initial visit to Moody, I trial-taught two classes. I was invited to teach Psalm 23 and 42 in an Old Testament class whose regular teacher was Dr. G. Coleman Luck. I took the whole hour to teach Psalm 23, and was about to begin Psalm 42 when the bell rang, and all the students got up and left the class-room for their next class! (They had only 5 minutes between classes at the time.) I was shocked, but learned early on that I must pace myself carefully in order to complete the lesson in the allotted time. Later that day, I taught 2 Timothy 3 for Dr. David Gotaas. Both teachers were most cordial, and the Lord gave me a sense of ease with the students. They asked a number of questions, some of them difficult. I began to realize how much I had yet to learn!

That evening I attended the 6th annual Evening School banquet for graduating seniors. The testimonies of the graduates were inspiring! As he bade me goodbye, Dr. Martin said he would give a favorable report to the Board, but I must also make my own decision if offered a position. He said he liked my teaching, although there was room for improvement (to which I heartily agreed). I wrote in my diary, "Oh, may God direct me clearly in this, one of the most crucial decisions I will ever make! God forbid that I should miss His good leading!"

C. Another School Shows Interest

That afternoon I was surprised when the weather suddenly shifted from summer to winter, dropping about 25 degrees. I would soon learn that this was not a rare phenomenon in Chicago! I left for California the next morning after a huge thunderstorm, amidst warnings of tornados. Soon after arriving, I returned a call awaiting me from another Bible Institute. I had written them also, asking about openings for teaching. They never replied, but I learned later that they had sent a scout to "spy out the land" when I taught the Maranatha Class at the Church of the Open Door. This school also wanted me to visit their campus and trial-teach before I made my final decision. But I greatly preferred the ethical way that Moody had dealt with me, as contrasted with the cloak-and-dagger tactics this second school had used. I struggled a whole week before making my final decision that, if invited, I would teach at Moody. (I preferred to get my doctor's degree first, so that I would not be burdened with the responsibility of completing it during my first year of teaching.) The very next day (May 16, 1963), after I settled the matter before the Lord, I received a call from Dr. Martin in Chicago, inviting me to become a member of faculty! I was filled with joy and accepted without hesitation!

D. Oral Exam Disaster

Ten days prior to that call, I had taken my oral exam for my doctorate at Dallas Seminary. I headlined my diary for May 6, "Blue Monday; Day of Disaster." The reason? I failed the exam! A well-meaning friend had told me the year before, "Don't bother to study for it; it's a snap!" What neither of us knew was that Dallas had stiffened up its oral exam after my friend took his, and it definitely was no longer a snap—it snapped me instead! That was easily the worst day of my life! I was totally crushed and depressed, thinking this was the end of my teaching opportunity. I had already been invited to Moody to be interviewed for a position there, and I was counting on passing the exam. Dr. Ryrie, who led the exam, said my dissertation was one of the best he had ever read, and all of the examining committee were surprised that I did poorly on the oral exam. Besides Dr. Ryrie, the committee included Dr. Walvoord, Dr. Witmer, and Dr. Dollar. The Dallas faculty graciously gave me another crack at the exam, to be taken a year later. When I phoned Dr. Martin at Moody and told him the bad news, he asked me to come for interviews anyway! I shall forever be grateful! That summer, I kept an intensive schedule of review for my oral exam and preparation for the classes I would be teaching at Moody. When I took the exam a second time in August 1964, I was prepared and did very well. Dr. Martin had graciously excused me from teaching summer school that year so I could prepare without distraction. Sumner Wemp, in an act of personal sacrifice, gave up his summer vacation so he could substitute for the classes I was to teach. I have never forgotten that kindness.

E. Added Reasons for Choosing Moody

In August of 1963 I took my old '54 Ford coupe and headed for Chicago. Why was I coming to Moody to teach, rather than some other school? For about ten years prior to that, I had been watching trends in Christian institutions. I had observed that Bible Institutes had produced more committed and spiritually mature Christian workers than had most other schools. Though each type of school is needed (Bible colleges, Christian liberal arts colleges, Christian universities, Christian graduate schools, and seminaries), a Bible Institute had something distinct to offer with its solid Bible-centered curriculum. Moody taught most of the books of the Bible, as well as thorough preparation in systematic theology. Further, Moody had the reputation of being the finest and oldest (or perhaps second oldest) Bible Institute in the nation. I had talked with many alumni, observed their effective Christian service, and noted that every one of them, without exception, had good things to say about MBI.

F. My First Apartment

My traveling companion on this overland trip to Chicago was Art Goldberg, a Messianic Jew who was a young married man and returning to Moody for his second year. We became good friends during the trip. Upon arrival, I stayed at the Lawson YMCA on Chicago Avenue near Dearborn Street for a few days, until I rented the first apartment I looked at, in west suburban Melrose Park. It was a new apartment, with 3 1/2 rooms, gas range, refrigerator, and free utilities except electricity. It rented for $120 a month. They called it a "garden apartment," but there really was no garden. It was simply a half floor below ground level. The apartment was about thirty minutes away from Moody Bible Institute by car. One of the fringe benefits was waking up to the lovely aroma of freshly baked bread wafting my way from a large Jewel bakery a block away. When my furniture arrived from California, I had a kitchen table with four chairs, a bed, and about two thousand books. The living room was bare except for one chair. I had to borrow over $500 from Moody to pay the van charges. This was an advance on my salary! It was only later that I learned that the community I had moved into was noted for its Italian Mafia activities!

G. Early Impressions of Chicago

The skyline of Chicago was truly beautiful, especially at night from the lakefront. People in the Midwest were friendly, and they would talk to strangers even in the big city. The business climate was stimulating. There were very interesting things to see and do in Chicago. The "El" intrigued me. This was the elevated train run by the Chicago Transit Authority. I had never before seen a train that operated about twenty feet above the auto and pedestrian traffic and ran in a rectangle around the downtown area (called the Loop). I later learned that it went underground in tunnels as well. I remember my first ride on the "El" train that went through a subway tunnel. The tunnel was like the darkest night, and I heard this tremendous roar and saw the blue streaks like lightening (caused by brushes making electrical contact with the "hot rail"). I was so frightened I thought I was going to die!

The first week of my arrival in Chicagoland, I visited Navy Pier, Moody Memorial Church (a sister institution with a common founder but not affiliated with the Moody Bible Institute), the Wheaton Bible Church, and the Brookfield Zoo. At Navy Pier, I was fascinated by the big freighters loading and unloading cargo from all over the world.

I liked three of the seasons in Chicago, spring, summer, and fall, but I came to hate winter, and still do. By contrast, Southern California hardly has seasons at all, and the leaves don't turn pretty colors in the fall. Sometimes Chicago's spring seems to get left out, moving suddenly from winter to summer. I wrote in my diary on April 24, 1980, "Tuesday was summer; Wednesday was spring; today is winter. So much for Chicago weather!"

A couple of situations precipitated a negative note in my diary: "Chicago has the highest rents, the rudest drivers, and the most foolhardy pedestrians I've ever seen! The pedestrians cross the street against red lights, with cars zooming all around them. They [pedestrians] must think they're angels, with non-material bodies that cars cannot harm! Perhaps this explains why Cook County Hospital is the largest in the world! I stopped for two male pedestrians, and they looked aghast, scanned my out-of-state license plate, and waived their surprised thanks." It was a shocking contrast with auto traffic in Southern California, where a pedestrian has only to step off the curb and all the drivers stop! (The liability laws are different in the two states.)

H. My Office at MBI

My new office at Moody was in 210 Fitzwater Hall, at the west end of the second floor. I kept that same office for 29 years! The layout was only about seven feet by nine feet, and eventually, my books were stacked clear to the ceiling. My desk almost blocked the doorway, and upon entering the office I had to make a hairpin turn to get behind the desk. I even made a wooden bookshelf to supplement the six gray steel shelves that lined three walls. I think I had the second-largest number of books in the office of anyone on the faculty. I have always loved to read, and I did read voraciously, especially during the first decade of my Moody career. I have even dreamed of being buried in a library!

My view of Wells Street out of my office window was anything but inspiring. Across the street was a business that renovated antique light fixtures. Antiques have never appealed to me. The building was a dingy gray, but had a couple of large display windows. Wealthy people would park their cars in front of the building and purchase elaborate fixtures for their mansions. Now and then I would see pedestrians on the sidewalk below. But my desk was arranged so that my back was toward the window. Books and students interested me much more than these surroundings.

J. Early Teaching Efforts

Before the school year began, five of us new teachers met with Dr. Martin for orientation. The other four were Dr. Bob Goddard (Bible), Rosemary Turner (Missions), Wilbur Aulie (Missions), and Omar Brubaker (Christian Education). They all became my good friends. In fact, one of the nicest features of my teaching career at Moody was the friendship I enjoyed among faculty, staff, students and employees. (There were some 500 employees when I first came to the Institute.) The faculty numbered around seventy, and the student body, about 700. The Moody Bible Institute really became my extended Christian family.

On September 10, 1963, with fear and trembling, I taught my very first class at Moody as a new faculty member. It was in Personal Evangelism, and I had 85 students, and they were "a fine, enthusiastic group." My second class was in New Testament Synthesis (Survey), and the students tended to be sleepy at one o'clock, right after lunch. I wrote, "It will be hard to keep their interest at that unhappy hour." I also had an Evening School class called the Doctrine of Man and Salvation. Teaching Evening School was required of each teacher as a regular part of his or her load until the fall of 1977, when it became optional with extra pay. Teachers were also required to be willing to teach Summer School whenever their services were needed. Summer School, if assigned, was also a regular part of the teacher's load with no extra pay until it was announced in the fall of 1970 that Summer School would become optional with an extra bonus! This announcement was a great encouragement to me, since I needed about two months every summer to revise day school course work and plan for fall classes. The other month was typically used for our house maintenance, repairs, and building projects and sometimes, a one or two-week vacation. And so, I stopped teaching summer school as soon as I was given a choice.

During a new teacher's first year, he or she is desperately trying to survive by staying a step ahead of the students. The teacher hopes that the students will not ask too many questions, because the teacher's knowledge reservoir is rather sparse. At first, I used to promise a student who asked a question for which I had no answer, that I would come up with an answer and get back to him or her. For example, a student might ask, "Do you think the apostle Paul wrote the book of Hebrews?" But I soon learned that it was acceptable not to know all the answers, and as I grew in self-confidence, I was able to tell the students honestly that I did not know; nor did I promise to find out. I had more than enough to do without any extra research projects! When a teacher wishes to impress, it is hard to be perfectly honest, and the students soon learn who is for real and who is bluffing! They appreciate authenticity, even if it is imperfect.

The second round in teaching the same course goes better, but there are still gaps to be filled in. When a teacher goes through the same course a third time, normally he or she has gained proficiency and self-confidence in the subject matter, and begins to feel comfortable in teaching the class. The teaching experience can gradually shift from mastering the subject to more personally relating to the students. Students have to be patient with new teachers, but if they can put up with them that first year or two, the student-teacher relationship becomes a lot more enjoyable and the education more profitable.

K. Carpool Friends Warn of Winter

Two carpool friends in that first year were Herbert Klingbeil, Director of the Correspondence School (later part of External Studies and more recently incorporated into the Distance Learning Center), and Charles ("Chuck") Christiansen, who taught public speaking and communications subjects. Chuck's main claim to fame at that time was as "Sailor Sam," the lead character in a radio drama by that name on WMBI. Kids and adults alike loved the weekly program. I had come from California with no overcoat, boots, hat, or scarf, and it was now fall, with winter coming soon. Herb and Chuck warned me, "Paul, you'd better get some winter clothing; it snows a lot and winter is really cold." I had no clue about how right they were. I was used to Southern California winters that seldom dipped below freezing. On my birthday, November 30, I walked two blocks to mail a letter. The weather was cold and windy, and I still had no equipment for winter. On that day, I experienced a double whammy— a severe sinus infection and a stomach flu that put me in bed for two weeks. The students started a rumor that I couldn't handle Chicago weather and would probably return to California, but they were wrong!

It was a very sad occasion three years later when Herbert Klingbeil passed away from a malignant brain tumor! He had been my head usher at our wedding, and a good friend and confidant.

L. Doctoral Work Completed

In July 1964, I flew to Dallas to re-take my oral exam for the doctorate. I wrote in my diary, "Dr. Waltke, Dr. Ryrie, Dr. Walvoord and Dr. Witmer were my 'tormentors.' I almost found myself enjoying the experience! All were most gracious and friendly." I knew that many of my friends at Moody were praying for me. I passed the exam this time with no difficulty. Finally my doctoral work was complete! I was so happy, I sent a telegram to Dr. Martin and my colleagues at Moody: "Oral passed; thanks to all for praying." The Western Union operator remarked, "You haven't used up all your words yet; would you like to say anything else about the funeral?" (In the South, Oral is a common first name.) But this was no funeral; it was a celebration! I have often re-told this story in my hermeneutics classes to illustrate the importance of knowing the context of a statement. I knew the context; the Western Union operator didn't. The result? A quite comical misunderstanding of the message!

CHAPTER 2
TEACHER AS MARRIED MAN

A. Dating

I had dated a number of young women while I was still in California, but none of these relationships matured into marriage. When I came to Moody as a teacher, I was the only single full-time member of faculty. I knew nothing about men's fashions. (I still don't!) I sometimes wore red socks to class with my dress shoes. A couple of times, I even wore shoes that didn't match! (I often dressed in the dark to protect my privacy; unfortunately, it also protected me from seeing what I put on!) At 30, I was seriously looking for a wife! At first, I dated an employee, but that went nowhere. Then I began dating a fellow teacher, but by my third date I learned that she was seven years my senior, and so I quietly dropped out. Next, I dated another employee named Mary, who worked for the Correspondence School. She must have wondered about my motives one Sunday when I took her with me to preach at a church south of Chicago. After leaving the church, I drove for an hour, only to pass the same church again! (I get lost easily when I'm driving, especially if I'm conversing at the same time!) After several months, our relationship deepened, and I found myself in love! I proposed, she accepted, and we were engaged—for one week! Then she called me on the phone and broke the engagement! She said I was a fine person, and she really liked me, but she just did not feel comfortable marrying at this time. I had a faculty friend, James Harrison, whose office was across from mine, and he later confided that he prayed daily that I would make the right choice in marriage. Mary was a fine young lady, but she had responded in an on-again, off-again way during our months of dating. Many of her interests were different from mine. Later, I became grateful that we did not get married, because it would have been a serious mistake. We were both genuinely seeking God's guidance, and he led in a way I had not expected. I was heart-broken, but I did recover emotionally after about five weeks. This was in the spring of 1964.

On Saturday, June 13, 1964, I attended the wedding of two of my students at Cicero Bible Church. William "Bill" Currie, the pastor, performed the lovely ceremony. Bill and I later became good friends. The usher seated me on one side of Miss Angela Dantuma, Dean of Women at Moody, and he seated Carol Ashby, one of my second semester students in hermeneutics, on her other side. I did not know that Carol was coming to this wedding, but she happened to know the young couple also. The couple were Susan Allen and Judson Clements, and we have kept in touch ever since. They are still missionaries in Tanzania. This was the first wedding I had attended in 20 years! When they gave me a bag of rice to toss, I thought it was to take home and cook!

After the wedding, I found myself giving Carol a ride back to the Institute, along with a new summer school student. As it worked out, Carol sat in the middle between the student and me! As Carol got acquainted with the student, she told him that, after high school in central Illinois, she had moved to Chicago to work four years as a reservationist, first for Capital Airlines, then for United Airlines. This was before she became a student at Moody Bible Institute. In my diary I wrote, "This would make her about 24 years old and put her hat in the ring [for potential dates]! I am much impressed with her friendliness, her wholesome smile, and her helpful, thoughtful disposition. I shall pray about this." The rest of the day I should have been reviewing my messages for a small church near the Indiana border where I would preach on Sunday. But instead, I mused over the question, "Should I ask Carol for a date, or should I not?" After all, Carol was a student, and I had never tried dating a student before. I wasn't sure what the Moody administration would think of it. This was delicate ground.

By Monday I had made up my mind. I would try it! So I pulled rank and sent a note to her via Moody's Central Post Office. The note requested that she come to my office that afternoon. While I was going through the lunch line in the Sweet Shop, where Carol had a job punching the cash register, I asked her if she had received my note. She said "No," so I told her what it said. She didn't know what to make of it. She wondered what she had done now! Was it her hermeneutics course? (She got a grade of C after running a B until my bear of a final exam!) Had she been too forward in asking me for a ride from the wedding? (She later confided that she had let one ride go, preferring to ride with me!) Did I want her to do typing for me? (She knew she didn't have time for that!) It never crossed her mind that I would ask her for a date!

Carol wore a nice blue dress when she came to my office after work. I was resting my head on my arms and taking a short nap, as I was weary with studying for my oral exam at Dallas Seminary. She came through the open door of my office and asked me if I was asleep. We both laughed when I said "No." Then she volunteered, "I don't know about you, but when I read for a long time I go to sleep!" I've never been enough of a socializer to enjoy small talk, so I just leaned back in my swivel office chair, and blurted out, "How would you like to go with me to the White Sox game this Friday night?" Carol sat down nervously on the student chair across from my desk. "Oh, that would be very nice!" she said. She was so surprised, she didn't know whether to laugh or to cry!

When Friday came, I took Carol to the White Sox game. We'd no sooner gotten inside the old, original Comiskey Park stadium than it began to rain hard. We waited beneath my umbrella for two hours or more, and they called the game off. But meanwhile, we had a wonderful visit, and got better acquainted with one another. I learned that Carol had three brothers and three sisters, was next to the youngest sibling, and lived on a farm three and a half miles west of Modesto, Illinois, a tiny town of 200 population, 35 miles southwest of Springfield. As a summer school student, she was then a floor counselor in Houghton Hall (the single women's dorm). I also noted in my diary, "She's really beautiful and radiantly happy in the Lord. What more do you want?" We still had ticket stubs, which served as rain checks after the game was called off. Carol was reasoning to herself, "I have this rain check in my hand. If he wants to invite someone else next Monday, he'll have to ask for it back." But I did invite her to come with me to the game to be played on the following Monday. At 6 p.m. I called her from my office and cancelled the date, because a terrific rainstorm was coming through. I did assure her that I would take her out another time. But by 7 p.m. the storm had vanished as quickly as it had come. I called Comiskey Park and they said they would play ball. So I called Carol again and reinstated our date. Between the two calls, Carol had changed to her grubbies, gone to the plaza on top of Houghton Hall, and was playing in the water there with other girls. Her hair, she says, was a mess. I explained to her the new plan and asked if she could be ready in ten minutes? She thought I was calling from my apartment in Melrose Park, but I was still in my office at Moody. "Fifteen?" she asked. I agreed and I picked her up in fifteen minutes. When we got to the parking lot of the ballpark, there were puddles everywhere. Carol lifted one foot and suspended it in the air for a moment before jumping over a puddle. She afterwards explained, "I know that didn't look very graceful, but I have a hole in one shoe, and I've forgotten which one it is." I replied, "That's alright; I have a hole in **both** of my shoes!" And I did!

For our third date on a Sunday night in June 1964, we took in the Melody Four Quartet at Moody's Sunday Night Sing. This tradition was a good opportunity for Christians all over Chicagoland to socialize, sing together, and hear some of the best musical talent. It was later changed to Friday Night Sing, and eventually held just once a month instead of weekly. It was done in Torrey-Gray Auditorium until the meeting got too large, and was moved to Moody Memorial Church. I wrote Carol a note the next day that said in part, "I just want to say how very much I enjoyed our previous dates, and how highly I regard you. Your Christian character, genuine interest in the things of the Lord, obvious joy, outstanding personality, and wholesome and mature attitudes have impressed me deeply." What Carol probably did not realize was that she had passed my initial test for an ideal wife. (I kept a list of desirable qualities in my billfold, which I reviewed every now and then, and she fulfilled nearly all of them!)

After passing my oral exam in Dallas (July 17, 1964), I flew to California to visit my mother. I really missed Carol, and we wrote each other every day while I was in California. I had already fallen hopelessly in love! I still cherish those letters! While still in California, I wired a dozen red roses to Carol at Moody. Her friends came to the Sweet Shop and told her there were flowers for her at her dorm door and that they were from me. She thought they were kidding. "But who are they *really* from?" she asked. When she saw the card, it read, "There is no special occasion, but you are occasion enough! [Signed] Paul" She says she was overwhelmed! The next day as I wrote Carol, I told her I was beginning to love her. I confided to my diary, "Lord, have mercy—I believe I'm hooked! Fine!"

A few days later, while attending a Campus Crusade conference on evangelism in San Bernardino, California, I received three letters from Carol. She had now told me plainly that she loved me too! I got busy planning our honeymoon even before I proposed to her! Dr. Willard Aldrich, president of Multnomah School of the Bible in Portland, Oregon, had recently re-married after being widowed. He told me about a cluster of six cabins at the Lonesome Cove Resort on San Juan Island, in the State of Washington. He and his new wife had spent a week or two there. It was located in the Puget Sound, with beautiful evergreens all around and the ocean nearby. There was only one catch: the place was so popular that you had to make reservations a year ahead of occupancy. It sounded like Eden to me, so I quickly reserved a cabin for a week in the following summer! I confirmed this reservation in the fall after our engagement.

On our ninth date, on August 7, 1964, Carol and I visited the Buckingham Fountain and the beautiful rose garden in Grant Park, downtown Chicago. We had earlier attended the All-Stars vs. Chicago Bears football game in Soldier Field. The Bears won, 28-17. I won, too, for while we were in the rose garden, I put my arm around Carol, kissed her for the first time, and told her, "I love you, Carol."

That August, when, because there was no school in session, the usual dating rules did not apply to the students at Moody (seeking permission of the dean, curfew, etc.), I had nineteen dates with Carol. (For younger readers, a date is not the same as just "hanging out." It is an agreement between a young man and a young woman where there is potential or real romantic interest to go someplace together and engage in some previously agreed upon social activity.) It requires planning and a considerable investment of time and usually, of money as well. Some might think we had a whirlwind courtship, and perhaps we did. But we were both of mature age (she was 23, I was 31) and we knew what we were looking for. When we found it in each other, we did not let any grass grow under our feet! Food poisoning from a Chicago hotel restaurant laid me up for two or three nights, and we were both too tired to go out on a couple of nights. One night I wrote out 37 reasons why I love Carol and gave it to her.

One Saturday morning in August, I spent several hours cleaning my apartment in Melrose Park, Illinois. In the living room I had only a cot and a single chair. The Fuller Brush Company's door-to-door salesman delivered some goods I had ordered. I invited him into the living room and offered, "Have *the* chair." He remarked with surprise, "I see you really go in for light housekeeping!"

On Sunday, August 16, 1964, I took Carol with me to Zion, Illinois, where I preached both morning and evening. We were hosted by a lovely couple who took us on a guided tour of Zion, and Kenosha, Wisconsin. We got back to Chicago late (1:15 a.m.) and I sat with Carol on a battered old sofa in the lounge of Osborne Hall, an old building on the east side of La Salle Street across from Torrey-Gray Auditorium. Moody Bible Institute owned Osborne as an auxiliary dorm. At 1:45 Monday morning, I proposed to Carol on our sixteenth date, and she accepted instantly! That was August 17, 1964. We visited until about 4:00 a.m. We were so happy we felt we *must* tell someone, but no one but the Crowell Hall night desk attendant was awake! So we told him, and he congratulated us.

Back in my apartment, after a few hours of sleep, I was musing about Carol's very modest economic background. She had to support herself completely in school, and her wardrobe was sparse, since her parents were too poor to help. So I wrote her a little poem:

"Gingham or silk, cotton or wool,

Fur coat or plain dress,

straight skirt or full,

Pink, red or black, white, navy blue,

Be it fancy or humble,

I'll always love you!"

On the first day of September I talked with Dr. Martin, my boss, for an hour and a half, and told him of our engagement, asked for some pre-marital counseling sessions, and asked him to perform the ceremony the following summer. He was delighted, and advised us to make a public announcement of our engagement immediately. I admit I was being a bit political, since I wanted the administration at Moody to approve our plans! After all, no other Moody faculty member that we knew of had ever married a full-time day school student at Moody, so we were concerned as to how this would fly!

Three days later, we ordered a diamond ring that cost $171.00 including tax! We also visited the Palmer House, and bought a huge fake ring made of glass. We decided to play a little joke on our friends. This pretend diamond was the size of a small apricot! I met with Carol when she had her coffee break in the morning. The Sweet Shop was humming with excitement, since Carol's fellow employees thought I was going to present her with her diamond ring right there! As a teaser, they swarmed around us, and even called on faculty member Donald Smith to peek through the window from the outside. Some students were also spying outside the window with the encouragement of Karen Shoesmith, one of Carol's friends who worked in the Sweet Shop with her. Then everyone shut the dividers in the back of the Sweet Shop where we were seated and scampered, leaving us a few moments of privacy. I pulled out my fake diamond and slipped it on Carol's finger. Then the fun began as Carol showed the ring dramatically to all the Sweet

Shop employees. Some of them nearly hemorrhaged while laughing! Karen Shoesmith laughed so hard, she had to wipe away the tears with her towel! What a surprise to everyone, and what a riot! Carol showed "the rock" to about fifty people during her work at the cash register in the Sweet Shop, including several faculty members. She even showed it to the dean of students, Frank Broman. The real ring was on order, but we wanted everyone to know that we were engaged!

The next day, I wrote Carol a more elaborate love poem that reflected on our first kiss. I called it, "How Transient Are Life's Earthly Things":

We walked the garden, hand in

hand, upon a moonlit night.

That eve she wore a bright red dress,

and she was draped in loveliness,

So warm, responsive, bright.

I could not shun the strong desire,

nor smother love's sweet flame,

And soon, my arm moved into space,

and gently, quickly found its place

About her charming frame

I whispered four amazing words, yet
 simple words to hear.
She quivered with emotion deep as
 we embraced; 'Twas Cupid's leap!
The words: I love you, dear!

She saw a lovely red, red rose, and
 put it to her cheek.
It was much like the dozen flowers
 she'd gazed upon for hours and
 hours—
My gift to her last week.

A month had passed. We found
 ourselves within the garden again.
In vain we looked for that red rose!
 How foolish for us
To suppose it would be waiting then.

How transient are life's earthly
things, they come and go so soon.
But love abides all earthly change,
unlike the flowers that disarrange
And quickly fade in bloom.

For God abides, and God is love, and
if our love's in Him,
'Twill never fade, for God's arrayed
in glory never dim.

As various faculty colleagues heard of our engagement, many of them came to my office to congratulate me. Carol's friends also congratulated her. I taught a high school Sunday school class at the Moody Memorial Church at the time, and Carol gave her testimony and news of our engagement to the opening exercises. (Opening exercises were held for each Sunday school department for inspiration and announcements before individual classes met.) The kids clapped their approval. As the news of our engagement spread around the MBI campus, lots of faculty members and students came to my office or sought out Carol in order to congratulate us. One morning, as Carol and I had our habitual coffee break together in the Sweet Shop, a group of my faculty friends drew their chairs around our table to interrupt our privacy, as a joke!

In September 1964, while I was still in a bit of a swoon because of our engagement, I began my second fall semester of teaching at Moody with a hilarious mistake. We had a tradition at that time to begin each class with a hymn or gospel song. I rushed to class and led the opening song, only to find that I was in the wrong classroom, a class taught by my colleague, Dr. David Gotaas! The next day I got a traffic ticket at Wells and Erie Streets, near MBI. The policeman informed me that I had run a stop sign! Isn't love wonderful?

During our engagement period, Carol and I continued to date, though many of our times together were less formal. One of our dates took us to Chicago's main fire station, built at the site (Jefferson and De Koven Streets) where Mrs. O'Leary's cow was said to have kicked over a milking lantern and started the great Chicago fire of 1871. We had visits to the Chicago Historical Society, the Field Museum, the Museum of Science and Industry, a medical museum, a folk fair, lots of restaurants, Rockefeller Chapel at the University of Chicago, Lincoln Park Zoo, Brookfield Zoo, faculty homes, sporting events, the Zion, Illinois Passion Play, and many other fascinating sites in the Chicago area. One never runs out of interesting things to see and do in Chicago!

Moody Bible Institute put on some fantastic musical programs, such as Handel's *The Messiah* and Candlelight Carols. One year in my diary I described Candlelight Carols as "lovely beyond description." But there were a few accidents that lent humor to the production as well. One of the funniest things I ever saw was when the angel Gabriel climbed into the side of the mountain on stage after making his momentous announcement to Mary. The angel had disappeared, when suddenly he tumbled prostrate on the floor before our very eyes—white robe, white tennis shoes, and all!

During our engagement period, I baked a batch of cookies and gave them to Carol. She lived on the 9th floor of Houghton Hall. The cookies circulated throughout the floor, but there were not enough for all the girls. In return, I received a mock report card in which I got an A for flavor, appearance, texture, usefulness, and quality, but an F for quantity and size. To prevent famine on the 9th floor, I was advised to make a crateful of cookies with each cookie measuring 6 inches in diameter!

Since Carol and I were both on campus much of the time, it was convenient for us to have lunch together as well as coffee breaks. Sometimes she would bring me a treat at my office in the early evening, when most faculty members had gone home. I was always hungry, and I enjoyed whatever she picked up at the Sweet Shop where she worked. We spent more and more time together making wedding plans. Since Carol was struggling financially to pay her school bills and other living expenses, I helped her a bit with those during her entire second year.

During the months of our engagement, we sometimes studied together. We continued to go to interesting places and do fun things. We shopped together for the cloth from which Carol sewed her own wedding dress. The two of us planned our wedding ceremony. Dr. Martin generously gave me several evenings of pre-marital counseling and discussion. I also read several books about marriage. I wrote Carol an acrostic poem, with lines beginning with the letters spelling each month from February through July. I also wrote her other love poetry, like this one:

You Captivate My Heart, My Sweet!

I smiled at her with twinkle bright,

desiring to be near.

She laughed at me with eyes of love

that told me I was dear.

I love you darling, Carol mine with

eyes and hair of brown,

Your mischief and your loveliness,

your smile and even your frown

Are all my precious heritage, the gift from God above.

The transitory shifts in life can ne'er erase your love.

You captivate my heart, my Sweet! You take my breath away!

Let us with joy anticipate our coming nuptial day!

In May 1965, Carol flew with me to Dallas, where she witnessed my graduation with the doctor of theology degree from Dallas Theological Seminary. It was wonderful to have her with me! We slept in separate bedrooms at a former neighbor's house.

Carol and I spent a lot of time together sending out wedding invitations and shopping for wedding supplies. She enjoyed a couple of generous wedding showers sponsored by her friends. We gave informal invitations to my Day School students, but of course, most of them were scattered during summer vacation when our wedding took place. We visited the "Ashby clan" downstate. So impressed was I with Clarence, Carol's friendly father, that in my social awkwardness I later introduced Carol twice as Clarence! We shopped together for future household furnishings. I often took her with me to preaching engagements in the Greater Chicago area. We were frequently invited to the homes of faculty or employee friends for evening meals and good visits. This made us feel very much loved and at home in our "Moody Family." Our many friends were very generous and gave us numerous wedding gifts without the formality of a wedding shower. As the wedding neared, I got busier than ever and more absent-minded. I drove to MBI with a guest book, medicine, and other items on the fender of my car. When I discovered the loss, I drove immediately back to Melrose Park and retraced my route. I found things in my driveway, and on the road one to three blocks away, and the guest book a mile and a half from my apartment! Some pages had tire marks on them, but it was too late and I was too stingy to buy another. We left the book intact and had wedding guests write on the unsoiled pages!

B. Wedding

Finally, on July 31, 1995, wedding day arrived. I was running two hours behind, and drove on the expressway in "Old George" (a 1954 Ford coupe) with my plywood arch tied on top. (I built the arch to hide the unsightly microphones on the church platform.) I almost lost the arch in a big rainstorm! The large Ashby clan was waiting for us to arrive at the 4,000-seat Moody Memorial Church sanctuary. Everyone was scrambling with the final preparations. We could not locate the ring bearer's pillow, which I had mistakenly left in my car, and my car was parked a couple of miles away to avoid pranks from friends or relatives! So Donald Hopper went and retrieved the pillow. I also could not find my carnation, but it was in the dressing room where my head usher, Herbert Klingbeil, was waiting for me. One of the Ashbys brought along her sewing machine, and finished the hem of a bridesmaid's dress just before the wedding began! Carol's relatives were from the country, and Carol's father, Clarence, said that the aisle of Moody Church was the longest aisle he'd ever walked! We had about 160 guests at the wedding itself, which was lovely (especially the bride!). The Ashby ushers said they kept seating the guests and losing them in the huge sanctuary!

The reception had about 120 guests and was held at Campus Corner on the MBI campus, a mile to the south. Carol had made a large chalk drawing of a scenic country path, with the words, "In all thy ways acknowledge him, and he shall direct thy paths" (Prov. 3:6). This was hung on the wall behind the bridal party table.

Not only did I marry Carol, but at the same time acquired the Ashby family as my new extended family. Since the Nevin family were almost all in California, it was really nice to be welcomed to the Ashby family. Carol's parents had seven children and lots of grandchildren, so I quickly gained many in-laws. Since most of the Ashbys were only about four hours away from Chicago, we have visited with them on many occasions. One of the most enjoyable occasions was always the annual Ashby Reunion, held in July or August each summer, up to the present day.

C. Honeymoon

After we took a day to recover from the wedding bustle, we left on our honeymoon with "Old George" packed to the gills. Later, I learned that my barber on Chicago Avenue had prayed daily that "Old George" would make the long trip, and for good reason! I had planned the trip carefully, except for one thing: I made no provision for contingencies! We left about two hours late, and from there on we were a couple of hours late to every planned stop along the way for the whole month of August! I had kept the honeymoon destination a big secret, and so Carol kept trying to guess where we were going. We stopped in Modesto, Illinois and visited Mom and Dad Ashby briefly. The first day on the road took us to St. Claire, Missouri. The next day we stopped at Weatherford, Oklahoma, where we bought large, luscious malts, and put them in our serving tray. Being newlyweds, we sat down beside each other on the rest stop picnic table, and the table upturned and spilled our lovely malts all over the tray, the table, and on us! We extricated ourselves rather quickly. A turnpike maintenance crew was sitting nearby, and didn't know whether to laugh for fear of offending us. I said to Carol, "Don't just stand there; suck!" Immediately we both applied our straws and sipped up the malt still in the tray. By then we both were laughing.

We phoned twice to a farmer in Texas where we expected to stay next. First we said we'd be late for supper; then again to forget supper, we'd be there for breakfast instead. The next morning we phoned the farmer a third time, and said we'd arrive when we got there! We made it at 8:30 a.m. and got in on the second shift for breakfast. That night we stayed with the brother-in-law of one of my Dallas professors. He was very nice, but not much impressed when we missed meeting him where he was waiting on Route 66 for us. Supper was delayed an hour. The next day we slept in until 11 a.m., and had our breakfast while our host was having his lunch! So much for careful planning! That day we made it to Flagstaff, Arizona, to a Christian conference grounds and got a cheap room with no plumbing.

Heading the next day for Los Angeles, we stopped on the loose shale fill of the road shoulder between Flagstaff and Williams, Arizona, to take a picture. But we got stuck with tires spinning! A very kind Native American towed us out, using our tire chains. We had lunch in Needles, California, one of the hottest places in the U.S. Going in from the 115-120 degree heat and humidity to an air-conditioned café was too much for my tired bride, and she nearly fainted! I had to get her jacket from the car. She recovered the rest of the day with the help of ice water packs. (Our car had no air conditioning.)

That night we reached the Los Angeles area and I introduced Carol to my mother, who had been unable to make it to the wedding. My mother, who was about five feet, one inch tall, looked up at Carol and remarked to me, "You didn't tell me she was that tall!" After visiting my mother in San Dimas, California, and my brother, Frank, and talking with my brother, George on the telephone, we then met Carol's biological mother, Myrl Anderson Keenan. Myrl impressed me as a fun-loving, friendly person who was determined to squeeze as much enjoyment out of life as she could. She and her third husband, Al, took us to see "The Daily Breeze" newspaper office where she worked, then to Fisherman's wharf in Redondo Beach.

On Sunday we went to the great Church of the Open Door in Los Angeles where I had been very active for ten years, and introduced Carol to many dear friends. We went to Glendale to visit Forest Lawn Memorial Park, with its famous paintings of the crucifixion and the resurrection, and the Last Supper Window.

The next day, following beautiful coastal route 101, we stopped in Greenfield, CA and saw my oldest brother, Jack, and his two dogs, Bob and Junior. Jack was still single, living in a duplex with a thriving vegetable and flower garden. He loved fishing and hunting, and gave us six cans of salmon that he caught and canned himself. Moving on up the coast, we made it to beautiful Lake Shasta.

On August 11 we traveled from Mt. Shasta into Oregon to Crater Lake, which unfortunately, was shrouded in fog. From there we tooled to Eugene and Portland, Oregon, and finally, Vancouver, Washington to my friend, Dr. Aldrich's home. Carol finally learned the secret of our destination! She was thrilled and greatly relieved! After over-nighting at the Aldrich's lovely estate, we took the Washington State Ferry out of Anacortes to Friday Harbor in the San Juan Islands. There we had reserved one of six beautiful, rustic cabins overlooking the Puget Sound, with evergreen trees all around. We spent a relaxing six days there in that little paradise. Well, almost paradise. We did nearly drown in our little boat with outboard motor when the tide came in. Just in the nick of time, I learned to head the boat perpendicular to the waves! Although we had used our borrowed fishing equipment, by the time we returned we had caught nothing. With a little smirk, the resort owner remarked, "I thought sure there were plenty of fish in that ocean; they must have run out!" That evening, the resort owner took us out and taught us how to catch codfish. For the rest of our stay, we had more cod to eat than we knew what to do with. Cod for breakfast, cod for lunch, cod for supper. We got very tired of eating fish! On our last day at the resort, we took a ferry trip to Sidney, B.C., and a bus tour to beautiful Victoria. The multi-colored flowers, the land-scaping, and the architecture make it one of the loveliest cities I have ever seen!

Leaving San Juan Islands, we bought some fresh fruits and vegetables and put them with the cod and dry ice in our ice chest. (The cod was for my mother down in Southern California.) When we became hungry, we got out some cantaloupe and ate it; then some tomatoes. Everything tasted strange. Soon we were burping and hiccoughing uncontrollably. This seemed truly odd! Finally we realized that the carbon dioxide from the dry ice had penetrated all the fruits and vegetables in our ice chest!

We headed for Yosemite National Park and bedded down in a lovely motel. I was sick with a throat infection, and got the chills! This honeymoon was more of an adventure than I had bargained for! We had to replace the car's generator along the way, and had six flat tires. But Old George kept running! Yosemite proved to be as beautiful as people said it was.

The next day was Sunday, and I had the privilege of preaching at the Church of the Open Door in the evening service. My throat nearly gave out on me, and I was embarrassed at how bad I sounded because the service was broadcast over radio! On Monday and Tuesday we enjoyed a get-together with Talbot Seminary friends, a tour of Marineland of the Pacific ("a real whale of a show"), looking around San Dimas, and visiting my mother and brothers George and Frank and other relatives.

On August 25, we began the return trip to Chicago. We visited Grand Canyon National Park's south rim, which was magnificent. At Thoreau, NM, we tried to take a shortcut through Navajo country to see a seminary friend, but got lost and went seventy miles out of the way on some of the worst dirt roads I'd ever traveled. Part of the time no road was visible, and we wondered if we were just wandering through the desert. We nearly ran out of gas before finding a paved road again. Were we ever grateful! We stayed that night with friends at the Brethren Navajo Mission at Counselor, New Mexico.

In a crazed frenzy to catch up with our original itinerary, we left the next day at 2:00 a.m. We drove furiously for 23 hours, arriving at 2:00 a.m. in Green Forest, Arkansas, where we got our friends, the Feltons, out of bed. (We were supposed to have supper with them!) I had served as Leonard Felton's assistant pastor in Los Angeles a short time, and he had now founded the Mid-America Mission in the Ozarks. We traveled 900 miles in one day! Because I failed to leave room in my planning for delays, our honeymoon had become an exercise in survival! We did at least share the driving. Too exhausted to preach as scheduled on Sunday morning, we slept in until 11:00 a.m. After a warm visit with the Feltons, we left Monday morning and arrived at Carol's parents' farm in Modesto, Illinois, Monday evening, where we had an enjoyable visit with the Ashby clan. The next morning, August 31, we visited the Pleasant Hill Church and Cemetery in Virden, Illinois, where, amazingly enough, one of my ancestors is buried! And so our marriage renewed the links between California, Kansas, and Illinois! We finally arrived back at Chicago at 11 p.m. We had covered 8,000 miles, and "Old George" had become an oilcoholic! (We had to add a can of oil every time we stopped for gasoline!) But our very strenuous honeymoon schedule was completed! We planned to sell George to the car crusher that fall, but a man desperate for wheels bought George right at the entrance to the junkyard, and so George's fate was postponed!

D. Marriage Counseling

For about 18 months in 1982-83, Carol and I went to marriage counseling to deal with some of the emotional baggage we brought into our marriage, and some of the issues that surfaced from time to time. We made wonderful progress during counseling, since we both wanted our marriage to be the best possible, and we were both willing to work at it. Although we had a good marriage before we went to a counselor, we've had a better marriage ever since! One of the many things we learned during marital counseling is that conflict does not have to alienate a couple, but that it can be positive if dealt with appropriately. Instead of dumping emotional garbage on each other and running away, we learned to see a conflict through to a happy resolution. We also learned we needed to stop trying to force our mate into our own mould, but let each person be himself or herself, and love each other just as we are. It took us about 17 years to learn that simple but difficult lesson.

E. Carol's Education and Career

Carol graduated from Moody with a diploma in 1966. Early in our marriage, she took a few courses at the College of DuPage, but soon found it was too much when the children were small. So she waited a few years, and when the children were old enough she worked diligently at completing her undergraduate degrees. She graduated from George Williams College in Downers Grove, Illinois, with a B.S. in social work in 1981, then got her B.A. degree in Bible and Theology from Moody in 1982. As part of her master's work she did an internship in marriage and family counseling for

Tri-Cities Services in Geneva. Finally, Carol earned an M.A. in counseling and psychology from Wheaton Graduate School in 1985. This became a good foundation for her second career as a marriage and family counselor. She has excellent counseling skills, and put them to use in private practice a well as in several hospitals. Besides the usual marriage and family practice, she has worked with addictions, brain-injured, and psychiatric patients.

In 1988 Carol earned a certificate in drug and alcohol counseling from College of DuPage. She also became a part-time faculty member at College of DuPage in the Department of Human Services from 1991 to 1992.

Carol has done extensive marriage and family counseling from 1985 until 1998. She earned her license in marriage and family therapy by taking a certification exam for the State of Illinois in 1995. During the intervening years, Carol not only counseled individuals and couples, but sometimes teens and children as well. She did marriage and family counseling at Mercy Center Hospital, Aurora, Illinois, and later became director and marriage and family therapist at the Christian Counseling Center, Western Springs, Illinois, until 1992. Carol spent one year assisting in psychiatric rehabilitation by counseling head injury clients at Meadowbrook of Chicago, Park Ridge, Illinois. For four years (1992-96) she worked with in-patient mental patients as a psychiatric therapist at Rapha Treatment Centers, a Christian organization. This was at Riveredge Hospital, Forest Park, Illinois. Evangelical Child and Family Services, Wheaton, Illinois, also employed Carol part-time as a marriage and family therapist.

Carol was devastated when Rapha suddenly downsized her in August 1996. After a great deal of thought and prayer, she discovered her keen interest in business. Following two discouraging years of various temporary jobs in business-related areas, she finally located a full-time job in a business she loves. Since 1998, Carol has worked for New Directions Search in Wheaton, which locates candidates for executive jobs in the hard goods manufacturing industry. She began her employment at New Directions by doing Internet research. Now she is one of the vice presidents of the firm.

Carol still does a small amount of marriage and family counseling, but has shifted her emphasis more toward business, and also toward career counseling. Twice a year, Carol has been co-facilitator for the Career Transition Workshop, an eight-week series of supportive encouragement and job-hunting procedures for people who wish to change jobs or are unemployed. This service was begun by David Cox, an IBM retiree, and was offered through 2004 at our church. Other churches are beginning to duplicate the program as well.

CHAPTER 3
TEACHER AS STRUGGLER AND JUGGLER

A. Fighting the Snow in Chicagoland Winters!

On January 26 and 27, 1967, the Chicago area had its worst snowstorm in Illinois history! On January 26 it took three and two-thirds hours just to drive to school from Glen Ellyn. I missed my first two classes. Traffic on the Eisenhower Expressway slogged along at 5-10 miles per hour. It took another two hours to get back home. The next day I cancelled the car pool (my local road was filled with two feet of snow) and took the commuter train instead. I took two hours to get to school, only to learn that classes had been cancelled. (In those days, the administration did not announce class cancellations over WMBI, Moody's radio station, and sometimes, even the main desk attendant was not informed.) After visiting with about fifteen other professors who had made it to Moody, I caught a train for home. The train was an hour late, and took twice the usual time to reach Glen Ellyn. I spent seven hours going to Chicago and returning, with nothing accomplished. In Chicago, busses, trucks and cars were stalled everywhere, and they lay sprawled in every direction on the roads! All roads and expressways were closed until late on the second day of the storm. On the third day, a Saturday, I spent all morning and much of the afternoon shoveling snow out of our driveway.

The snowfall in Chicago in the winter of 1977-78 was a new record of 77.5 inches, just a half-inch greater than in 1969-70. The lowest temperature of which I am aware since I've lived in the Chicago area was –29 degrees on January 11, 1979. On January 15, 1979 I left the office at 6:45 p.m. and took the wrong train (northwest line instead of the west line). I got off at Jefferson Park and took a CTA train back to the loop. I finally arrived back at the Chicago Northwestern Station at 9:42, but no trains were running except sporadically, due to the heavy snows. I called Carol and decided to spend the night in my MBI office. I arrived back at Moody at 10:30 p.m., walking in the middle of the street, and slept on my cot from 11:00 p.m. to 8:00 a.m. It was quite an experience! The city sidewalks were covered with a yard of snow, and O'Hare Field was closed for several days. The next day, it took me over four hours just to get home. On January 19, we had more snow, and I had to stand in a thickly packed vestibule until the Lombard stop. Until Villa Park, more people got <u>on</u> the train than <u>off</u> of it at every stop. For the afternoon trip taking people home, this was unprecedented! In February 1979, Chicago broke the all-time snowfall record of 82 inches!

The *Chicago Tribune* for January 10, 1982, called it "the coldest day in history." It was -26 degrees Fahrenheit, with winds 23-33 miles per hour. It happened on a Sunday, and we couldn't start our car to go to church. We invited several neighbors, and had a church service in our house! But on January 20, 1985, another Sunday, the temperature went even lower, to –27 degrees officially. Neither of our cars would start, so our family had its own hour and a half church service in the living room. Unofficially, it turned –28 degrees on January 17, 1994 in West Chicago. Only one of our three cars would start that day.

I left school early in November 1985 to find a trooper's cap ("mad bomber's cap" to our kids!). I found one at a surplus store. Made of vinyl, it was a nightmare to look at, but it had a visor that protected my sinuses and forehead when it was cold and windy, and ear flaps to prevent ear infections. It also had fake fur for warmth. Although I was ashamed of the cap's appearance, it did enable me to walk through the worst of weather without getting too many respiratory infections.

B. Personal Health and Scheduling

Carol and I lived a hectic life of crisis scheduling the first few years of our marriage and far beyond, even during the heart of my teaching career. (One of my diary entries for October 1985, was "Rush, rush, rush. Tired, tired.") After we were newly married, she had a cumulative weariness from her two previous years of employment and study. She had often stayed up late with her homework. I became tired also as I had a frantic schedule of teaching, preparation, counseling students, preparing and correcting exams, grading, reading, reviewing books, preaching, taking extra courses at Roosevelt University with the thought of earning a master's degree in philosophy, and various social events. I was still young, and concerns about over- scheduling were overshadowed by my desire to be as fully prepared for teaching as possible. I also had the responsibility of helping to register evening school and summer school students. This was required as part of my regular workload. I frequently revised exams, quizzes, and class notes. Some of these notes were sold to my students in the bookstore. On Saturdays we both often slept in until 10 or later, assuming I would not be going to my Chicago office that day. However, I did work in the office on many a Saturday just to keep up with my work.

I was especially susceptible to getting the flu, and for perhaps the first fifteen years of my teaching career, I caught the flu once, twice, or even three times a year. Sometimes I would be in bed for several days, or even a week. While we were dating, I was sick with flu for four days, and Carol sent a box of groceries to my apartment via another faculty member. That proved to be a godsend, as I was too ill to go to the grocery store.

But the student perspective was quite different from mine. When a professor was ill, they could let his assignments slide for a while, and it was a nice break not to have to attend his classes. They had plenty to do without them, anyway! When Carol and I were engaged, Carol still lived in Houghton Hall, where she was a floor assistant. When I was ill, she would post on her dorm door a daily announcement of my condition and whether my class would meet that day. She had her door closed, but she could hear the women students as they pattered by her door, read the announcement that I was still ill and class would not meet. They would laugh happily and say, "Great!" before pitter-pattering back to their rooms! Meanwhile, Carol was feeling very sad!

We also worked furiously on house cleaning when we could squeeze in a bit of time, and Carol did much of her cooking for the coming week on Saturdays, especially the first year of our marriage, when she was finishing her third year for her Moody diploma.

All of this was in addition to our home church attendance and ministries. My workload required me to keep late hours. This meant frequently getting to bed after midnight, and arising very early. Too many times I got only four hours of sleep, and Carol did the same. I tried to pry all the activity out of a 24-hour day that it could possibly yield. I must admit that I was quite a workaholic. This attitude of work till you drop was instilled into me as a child, and I still have to battle it in my "mature" years! Such obsessive-compulsive behavior is not easily overcome, and the Moody environment did much to reinforce it. When Wayne Oates published his book, *Confessions of a Workaholic* in 1971, I bought it and eagerly devoured it. But only gradually did I learn to put its advice into practice. The harsh and ever-changing Chicago winters contributed nothing to my health, either. Moody is located just a few blocks west of Lake Michigan, and the "lake effect" brings snows and strong winds that make winter weather something to dread. My illnesses were costly in terms of missing classes and getting behind in correcting papers and counseling students. It was not unusual for me to take two or even three short naps during the day to try to prevent the flu from conquering my body. Many years passed before I learned that I could prevent this dreaded sickness by making eight hours of sleep a top priority.

Carol found it extremely frustrating to keep up her work as a third year student while functioning as a faculty wife and homemaker as well. She was so tired that, if she had not married, she might have dropped out a year to recuperate and earn money before returning for her third year.

During the first two years of our married life, Carol often came to school with me and helped with office tasks. That was a terrific assist! She would visit my classes, and after our children were born, she brought them to visit also. The students loved it! She also kept very busy cleaning house, washing clothes, ironing, cooking, sewing, baking, and entertaining guests. In addition, she taught Sunday school, attended the Women's Missionary and Prayer Circle at Moody, and the Faculty Wives' Fellowship. She helped with various church programs, such as Vacation Bible School and Primary Church and sometimes, with the nursery. Carol also corrected exams and homework papers for the Moody Correspondence School for a year or two, to earn a little extra money for our budget.

For many years, we put out what was at first a quarterly family letter to our relatives and friends; later it became semi-annual, and finally, an annual letter. In 1977, Carol became president of the Women's Fellowship at Pleasant Hill Community Church, in Wheaton, Illinois.

Beginning in 1967, each faculty member was given a student helper to do several hours of office work a week, depending upon the teacher's overall work load. Student helpers could correct "objective" exams, enter grades and absences manually, record absence excuses, help catalog books, run errands, and do other office chores where a teacher could use assistance. Sometimes students who worked for me would give me extra hours of work for free, just because they could see how far behind I was on clerical tasks. They sacrificed precious time to do this. This is part of the Moody spirit, and deeply appreciated!

Carol and I had short nights due to our hectic schedules, but we tried to take extra naps afterwards to recuperate. Once in a while, we went to bed in late afternoon or early evening when no crisis was pending. It was not unusual for me to arise at 3 a.m. or occasionally at 2 a.m., or, on other nights, to go to bed at midnight or 1 a.m. One of the most frequent remarks in my diary in those early years was how tired I was or how tired Carol was. For example, my diary for May 17, 1967 began, "Today I was tired; yesterday I was tired too, tomorrow I probably will still be tired!" The Lord was very gracious in protecting us from getting serious diseases despite inadequate rest. One Saturday I was upright but totally fatigued. (Saturdays were our day to do the extra household chores, maintenance, to fix things that didn't work, to work in the yard, etc.) I wrote of this Saturday [December 6, 1986]: "I really fell apart today. I was TOTALLY out of it! My major accomplishments were to sweep the workshop floor and to try for 2 hours—unsuccessfully—to balance the bank statement so I could pay bills! I couldn't say a straight sentence without garbling my words! I talked of the DAG BOSKET (dog basket) and cleaning the HUMILIATOR (humidifier)— which I never got to. It was hopeless and hilarious! Carol was also silly and so were our daughters. I gave up and went to bed at 10:30."

In 1968 I had a hearing test. I was told that my hearing was normal except for high tones, and that nothing could be done about it. Carol was not impressed with this report. She could detect some difficulties in my hearing, and these gradually worsened during my teaching career. In 1973 I took a written test on *Rules of the Road* to renew my license. The clerk asked if my hearing was satisfactory. I replied, "What?" One of the reasons I retired early at 62 was that I was having difficulty in hearing my students' questions in class. I also suffered many throat and sinus infections during my teaching years. For most of these, I just kept right on teaching until the infections became severe enough to be disabling. Sometimes I had sore throat and even laryngitis from post-nasal drip. But this condition largely cleared up after I had my tonsils removed, and later underwent surgery for a deviated septum.

In 1969, with the help of female faculty members, women's dormitory staff, counseling staff, and female students, Carol organized the Houghton Hall Helpers. The faculty wives (and later, other Moody employees) were encouraged to do special things with and for the women students and be an encouragement to them. A *Moody Student* (student newspaper) article noted that the faculty wives would each be assigned to a Houghton Hall floor and work with a student floor helper to provide refreshments, flowers, magazines, or favorite recipes. They would also invite female students to their homes from time to time, and remember them on their birthdays. This program was a real success, and led in time to including male students also. And so, Carol found herself heading up the Floor Parents' Program, in which she coordinated all the volunteer work for both men's and women's dormitories. This was an unpaid position, but a wonderful ministry to students! I found myself helping Carol recruit new floor parents at the beginning of quite a few semesters. Our special assignment was the fourth floor of Houghton Hall. Years later, we had a close relationship with the third floor of Culby (Culbertson Hall men). We did lots of special activities with these students. These included bringing flowers, helping decorate the fourth floor lounge, celebrating their birthdays, joining in their floor parties, inviting them out to our house, taking in cookies or cakes or candy, etc. I even made a cassette tape on femininity, to play at the fourth floor, Houghton Hall party in 1975! In 1980, Dean of Students Robert Irvin and the student body president presented Carol with a dozen roses and a lovely plaque to honor her eleven years of leadership in the Floor Parents' Program.

In 1988 I got my first pair of hearing aids. My hearing had been deteriorating for some years, and by now had reached a crisis. The hearing aids were not perfect, but they helped a great deal. I always had a struggle to keep my ears and the aids clear of wax accumulations. The aids amplified *all* sounds—not only the human voice, but also the sound of car tires on the road while driving, and even the sound of my teeth and jaws while eating! Sometimes the hearing aids squeaked while I chewed, and others sitting near me could hear them! At this writing I have worn out three pairs of hearing aids, and am now on my fourth.

On April 27, 1989, as I was nearly finished with my studies at Wheaton Graduate School, I had to run to catch a commuter train with a heavy overcoat and a loaded brief case. My right arm and leg went numb for a half-hour. I thought it was a pinched nerve, and took a series of about twenty chiropractic adjustments to correct it. I now believe it was my first heart attack and first stroke, rolled into one! Beginning in mid-May, I had severe stomachaches when I exerted myself physically, and I assumed I had the beginnings of an ulcer. The "ulcer" continued to worsen, and I visited my family doctor for treatment. On June 26 I took a stress test and failed it. The cardiologist told me I had already had a heart attack! This was quite a shock! Three days later, I was admitted to Central DuPage Hospital, less than two miles from our home. They kept me in the hospital for a week before I underwent quadruple bypass surgery, since they (and Carol) feared I might suffer another fatal heart attack if I were discharged! About one-fourth of my heart was immobile, so the damage was considerable. The prospect of surgery was harder on Carol than on me. She was quite worried and fearful, and she became very tired trying to visit me and do her own counseling work as well. I was encouraged by many visits from family and church and Moody friends, both before and after the seven-hour surgery, which took place July 7, 1989. Here are some of my impressions of hospital life: the dedicated nurses and competence of doctors, and the huge staff it takes to run a hospital; the countless blood samples needed for all kinds of tests; the embarrassment of a hospital gown; the constant interruptions from the nurses checking vitals; the dreaded midnight flashlight check after I finally succeeded against all odds to get to sleep despite the very noisy environment; the coming and going of roommates after an average two-day stay; the vacuity of most TV programs; the same cardiac diet tasting worse and worse each day; the smell of medicine and of my not-so-clean body. Most of all was the incredible weakness I had after surgery. I was finally released after sixteen long days. Going home was like going to heaven!

C. Teacher as Commuter

During the first four years of teaching, I was in a carpool to get to work. In 1966-67 I even did all the driving myself and was reimbursed by the other carpool members. But soon I learned that the commuter train (The Chicago and North Western) was a more pleasant and reliable way to go to work and return home again, usually right on time. The train was not ordinarily weather-dependent, and when we calculated the cost of gasoline and car repairs, it was actually cheaper. It also had the advantage of allowing the rider to rest, pray, or study without distraction. So I became a loyal train commuter for most of my teaching career. When we moved to West Chicago in 1969, it became a problem to make the 1.7-mile trip to the Winfield train station and back. Beginning in 1970, I rode my bike on Highlake Road to the station. As auto traffic increased, it became more and more dangerous for bicycles. A vehicle going 50 miles per hour on two occasions sideswiped my wire basket over the rear tire, though I did not fall off the bike either time. The first occurrence was in 1972 while I was riding westward against the sun. The driver didn't see me because of the sun in her eyes. She was so frightened by the accident that she nearly crashed while trying to stop. She offered to pay me damages, but I requested only $5.00 to replace my basket! If the basket had not been hit, it might have been my leg instead. The Lord's protection was most evident! The next day I learned that my brother, Robert, had been hit by a car and killed instantly in Southern California! The reason? The sun was in the driver's eyes and he did not see Robert at all! Here were two almost identical situations. My brother was killed, but I was spared. "Why?" I wondered. I decided that God had more work for me to do for him!

During the second auto/bike incident, my left little finger was broken by being hit by a right-hand mirror mounted on a van. My replaced basket was also smashed again! Evidently the driver did not know he had hit me, and never stopped. Nor did I discover until later that my finger had been broken. When I got home, I played the piano for visiting Moody students, broken finger and all!

Riding my bike in the winter was not fun. Sometimes the weather got so cold that the back of my overcoat became coated with ice because my breath floated backward and the moisture froze on my coat! On several occasions, due to icy roads, I slipped and fell to the pavement. There were other problems with biking— flat tires, spills on gravel, the chain coming lose from the sprocket, and especially, heavy traffic on Highlake Road, which was barely wide enough in each lane for a bicycle and a car side by side. For several years, I rode my bike in the morning, but had one of my family members pick up my bike and me in a car for the evening return. Finally, I gave up riding my bike to the train station, and asked Carol (or later, one of our children) to drive me to the station and pick me up in the evening. Sometimes I walked to or from the station, which took about 30 minutes. In January 1988 I wrote: "Took the 7:23 via car. I barely climbed aboard, jumping over a wooden fence, when the train door closed behind me! There's nothing so exciting as living dangerously!"

Over the years, I had some interesting experiences riding the train. During the twenty-eight years that I commuted by rail, there were perhaps a dozen occasions when the engine ran out of diesel fuel or the electrical generator broke down. This would cause a considerable delay of a half-hour to an hour. Commuters had to wait until another engine could hook up to the first one and pull or push us through the remainder of the route. For several summers, the engines' generators could not produce enough electricity to run the lights and the air conditioning simultaneously, especially on very hot days. This resulted in an electrical failure, during which the commuters were without fresh air or light for the rest of the trip. On one occasion, due to a switching error, the commuter train full of passengers ran onto a sidetrack and into the train yard, and suffered a long delay trying to exit the yard. During heavy snows or very cold weather, the switches between or beside the track broke down, resulting in an inability to complete the run into the Chicago station. Sometimes these switches had to be heated by building a fire next to them! To be fair, most of the breakdowns occurred in the 60's and 70's when equipment was wearing out. The 80's and 90's saw new engines and cars, and performance was greatly improved. On April 2, 1975, we had a 12-inch snow during a blizzard. On the afternoon westbound run, the train ahead of us hit a truck in Maywood, and the eastbound hit a car. Rush hour westbound trains were backed up all along the route. The train I was riding suffered a delay of nearly four hours while tracks were cleared! But I never suffered a train crash during all my years of train rides, and for this I am very thankful! The train that I was riding did hit and some-times kill commuters who were crossing the tracks. I would read about it the next day in the newspaper.

Once or twice every two to three years, the members of the rail-road unions would threaten a strike. Sometimes labor disputes involved train engineers, sometimes, conductors and collectors; at other times, a strike would be called in sympathy for freight workers or other railways. Usually the strikes were averted at the last moment, but now and then the strike was actually held. Strikes were trying for commuters, who had to find alternate transportation on a moment's notice. During these times, I either drove my car into Chicago, or else rode the Burlington Northern out of Naperville. Sometimes faculty members formed a hasty but temporary car pool.

There were still challenges after the train ride. Moody is located about a mile and a fourth (some 15 blocks) from the Chicago and

North Western Station at Madison and Canal Streets (now known as the Ogilvie Transportation Center). Some faculty members took a bus or rode the "El," but I preferred to walk, as did many other faculty members and other employees. While walking, we sometimes encountered stormy weather, but I learned to dress warmly when it was cold, rainy or windy. I also learned to listen to the weather report carefully and check the outdoor thermometer before leaving the house. Over the years I lost several umbrellas during heavy winds!

During less severe weather, I wore a felt hat for cool weather and a straw hat for warm weather. My hat sometimes blew off from strong wind and sailed down the sidewalk or out into the road. I usually retrieved it with little consequence, but one time my hat blew off and sailed into the Chicago River. I never recovered that one! Chicago was dubbed "the Windy City" because of long-winded political speeches, but it also accurately reflects its weather!

D. Nap Time

Soon after coming to Moody, I learned of "The Saints' Rest" (my name for it), a room set aside on the first floor of the Women's Guild Hall for men to rest on six or eight old metal cots during the noon hour or whenever they needed it. I made good use of this room until the building was torn down in 1970. I had a long-standing personal habit of taking a nap after lunch each day, begun in 1954 when I commuted to Talbot Seminary in Los Angeles. The nap was so refreshing, I felt I had begun a new day after each one, and this helped me to keep long work hours without excessive fatigue. It was also a circuit breaker for my workaholism. The women employees had a cot room in another part of the campus. When "The Saints' Rest" was no longer available, I bought a folding cot and kept it in my office. I made a sign, which read, "I am resting, sweetly resting. Please call again later" and placed it over the narrow window in my office door. Although I was occasionally disturbed by the telephone or by a student who ignored my sign, I usually got a good nap right in my office after eating a bag lunch consisting of a sandwich, fruit, veggies and a cookie or two. At other times I ate in the dining hall with the students.

E. Living Expenses and God's Provision

Through the years of my teaching at Moody, we always struggled with financial needs. We had a modest budget, and revised it at least once a year. For most of those years, I was the sole breadwinner, and we often wondered how we could possibly have enough to do all that we felt the Lord wanted us to do. This included generous giving to our church, to missionaries, and to other Christian ministries. It also included sacrificial tuition and other expenses to keep each of our children in Wheaton Christian Grammar School. (We feel it was well worth it.) When Tim was 9, we suggested to him that we might transfer him to public school. He was so upset that we even considered this, that we decided to trust the Lord for the tuition and keep him in the Christian school. In the grammar school, Joy went out for basketball and volleyball, played the flute, and sang in the school choir. Ruth was statistician for the girls' basketball team. We often bought used clothing for the children and even for ourselves. Later, the Repeat Boutique, a used clothing ministry operated by Wheaton Bible Church, became a lifesaver! Many diary entries were reminders that we had to scrape for basic living expenses, but we also noted in faith, "The Lord will provide." And he did! We were never without food or without a roof over our heads. (Sometimes the roof did leak, though!)

We always had at least one car to get around in. Up until 1978, each car in turn was second-hand and required many repairs to keep it running. Transportation was often inconvenient, but one way or another, we got to where we needed to go. We never had enough money to save any of it until my final five years or so at Moody. My greatest regret in this regard is that making do with what we had took a lot of time away from study and ministry. It left almost no time to write. But we did our best with what God provided, and I believe he was pleased with our lifestyle. In 1985 we had an especially hard time making ends meet, and prayed about it and entrusted it to the Lord. We were moved to tears when friends from our church presented us with a $400 check with a promise of another to come! I received a small salary increase nearly every year, and for this we were grateful.

F. Our Own House

On August 15, 1969, we closed on purchasing our first and only house in unincorporated West Chicago, some 32 miles west of the city. Marvin Beckman, Moody's attorney, was very helpful, and came out with me on the train to close the deal with the bank, going over all the papers to make sure they were correct. An anonymous friend of Moody had loaned us $3,000 for two-thirds of our down payment. It was an old frame house (we estimate it was built in the 1930's) with full basement and 4 small bedrooms, a tiny living room, a glassed-in porch, a kitchen, and one bathroom. The selling price of $17,900 was low, even for those days, but all we could afford. We even had to borrow the $1,500 to supplement our $3,000 loan from Moody to complete our down payment of $4,500, since we had no savings at all! I made a number of small improvements over many years, as time and money permitted.

An important addition was the building on of my personal office and library, which I needed after my retirement in 1995. That one room cost $30,000 in 1995, almost twice the price of the whole house in 1969! I built my own bookshelves for my library of 4,000 books, each of ten bookshelf units being 9' 4" tall! I thoroughly enjoy my library!

But the most important improvement of all was a nearly complete remodeling of the whole house, except for the basement. A competent contractor and his crew did this in four months during 1999-2000. Walls and ceilings were replaced, insulation added for the first time, new doors put in, the 22 windows replaced, an upstairs bathroom added, and new wallpaper and carpets installed. The old plumbing was almost completely replaced. New interior door and window frames were built. We also got a new furnace and new furnace ducts for the upstairs bedrooms, and added central air conditioning. All major appliances were replaced. It was like a new house! I painted the doors, windows, and trim to save money, which took me three months!

G. Teacher as Do-It-Yourselfer

Sometimes students think that teachers live a charmed life, with few trials and many joys. To set the record straight, I am offering here a little essay I wrote on the last day of 1963. It is entitled, "Don't Do It Yourself!"

"Have all you do-it-yourselfers done it yet?" read the sign in the hardware store. Whenever I think of that sign, I say to myself, "No, and I don't intend to, either!" To illustrate the follies of do-it-your-self-ism, take the case of the Ford car thermostat. I was getting tired of freezing to death in sub-zero weather in my '54 Ford coupe. It had a defective thermostat that kept the heater cold. I had been put off by overburdened mechanics who had big jobs to do, and didn't want to bother with my small job. So I gritted my chattering teeth and determined to install a new thermostat myself. "There's nothing to it," the mechanic told me. "Just unscrew these two bolts on the manifold and set the thermostat in."

My lone crescent wrench worked fine for disentangling the first bolt, but that second bolt was more resistant. The neck of my crescent was simply too thick to fit the tight spot, even after disconnecting two water hoses and going into all sorts of contortions. There was only one thing to do—I would have to walk to town (Melrose Park) in that c-o-l-d Chicago winter and buy a small wrench to fit this wicked nut.

In an hour I was back at the operating table, armed with an expensive socket set and a fistful of *metric* end wrenches that wouldn't fit a single nut on my Ford, except, perhaps, the nut behind the wheel! Happily, the socket set worked better, and the second nut gave up its grip remorsefully. Oh yes—a little item I had overlooked—draining the radiator! I was losing antifreeze, and the thirsty ice and snow on the ground were gulping it up fast. With a fleet of buckets, pots, and pans, I managed to collect most of the coolant to be used again when the surgery was completed. I inserted the new thermostat and drooled with the expectation of finishing the job quickly. I sewed up all the hose clamps and tightened all screws in sight, then started the motor. But what was that leak? During the operation, I had jarred a very rusty piece of tubing from the water pump, and no amount of hose tightening could stop the fatal gushing of antifreeze from the newly opened wound! Stuffing a piece of old newspaper into the gash, I was faced with another walk to the store to buy a new hose and clamps.

Finally the job was almost completed. All that remained was to buy two more quarts of antifreeze to replace what had escaped in the fray. Five hours and a pot of the neighbor's soup later, and $25.00 poorer, my car heater was working at last! The satisfaction of success helped remove the sting from the reality that I still had to clean my now-greasy topcoat, wash my blackened mittens in carbon tetrachloride, and re-scrub my newly mopped floors from the grease, mud, and slush I had tracked through the apartment.

So, in response to the hardware store sign, "Yes, this do-it-your-selfer has now done it—and had it!" It may be a long time before he does it again. But that is all wishful thinking. With limited income, teachers often have to do things themselves that professionals could do faster and better—but not cheaper. And so, throughout my teaching career at Moody, I have gotten involved in many do-it-yourself projects, including many hours of working on my own car (which all too often would not run; Chicago winters bring out the worst in a car); repairs around the house, yard maintenance, some interior remodeling, etc. In 1979 I made a list of 75 do-it-yourself projects around the house that needed implementing. Some of these were pleasant diversions from my more academic pursuits, but others required loads of precious time that drained away hours that should have been put into reading, preparation for teaching, and relating to my students, and later, my family.

In 1973 I built forms for a concrete slab on which I erected a steel tool shed purchased from the J. C. Penney's catalog. Since the floor was on a slope, I [foolishly] thought it necessary to fill in the deep end of the form with cement instead of dirt and gravel! An airline pilot friend helped me trowel the slab. The ready-mix man delivered 7 yards of cement, and told me that I had a foundation solid enough to erect the John Hancock Center upon it! (At this writing, the John Hancock Center, at 100 stories high near Chicago's lakefront, ranks sixteenth among the world's tallest buildings). This tool shed lasted for several years, only to be blown away by 75 mph winds! I replaced it with a wooden tool shed kit from a lumber company, and that tool shed is still in good condition some 29 years later.

For at least 26 years of my Moody career, Carol cut my hair to save money. Although I was skeptical at first, she did just as well as a barber would have done. She also cut Tim's hair when he was small. (Tim added, "I had no choice.")

On one occasion, Carol and I had to return a few soda pop bottles to buy groceries with the refund. Another time we had just one penny between us when payday rolled around. In 1969 I wrote in my diary, "Carol and I worked four hours on finances. Terrible, terrible, terrible! May the Lord supply." And God *always did* supply our needs, one way or the other!

The biggest do-it-yourself project I ever got into was repairing and thickening the concrete foundation of the house to stop the frequent flooding of the basement. (One night Carol and I mopped the basement three times!) The frame of the house rested in part on ten or twelve 6 x 6 posts, set right into the foundation. Unknown to us, before we bought the house, these posts had all rotted, leaving only a thin veneer of wood on the inside basement wall. Water poured right through whenever we had heavy rains.

We began the project in 1982, and it took us two years to complete. With pick and shovel we dug a ditch 3 feet wide and 6 feet deep around three sides of the house. We used a pulley system to bring up the buckets of soil from the ditch's bottom. We also used a borrowed electric jackhammer to break up huge rocks submerged under the heavy clay soil. Some rocks were as big as 30 inches across. Without the jackhammer we could never have removed them.

Our whole family got involved in digging on afternoons, evenings, Saturdays, and more extensively during two summers. We had Saturday volunteer help from our Sunday school and church friends, another Sunday school where I taught extensively, and from some of Tim's high school and church friends at various times. A number of Moody students came out on different Saturdays and helped dig. One of Tim's friends fell backward into the open dry well with the heavy electric jackhammer in his hands, but was unhurt, amazingly! One friend of the family, Wayne Braun, came many Saturdays on his motorcycle to help us dig. John Foos, a son of fellow faculty member Harold Foos, also helped a great deal. We paid John a small hourly wage. We had no money to hire a contractor, and even if we had, no contractor in his right mind would take on such a grim challenge! It was backbreaking work, and a sore trial to the muscles. Inside the basement, we built a temporary support system of 6 x 6 posts from floor to ceiling, to prevent the house from falling in! Carol and I dug throughout the second winter, never stopping for cold weather because we wanted so badly to finish the project!

Using a hammer drill, I made holes in the old foundation, which varied in thickness from six to nine inches. Into these holes we inserted long eye lag bolts. Through the bolts' eyes we placed iron reinforcement rods, pounding them into the ground. Then we laid horizontal rods across, and tied the intersections with wire. The purpose of all this was to anchor the new concrete foundation to the old one, so that the combined thickness would keep water out of the basement.

When the ditch was completed, I built forms of 3/4 inch plywood and 2 x 4's. I made a large wooden funnel so the concrete would go inside the forms. The ready-mix truck driver said our yard was the hardest place he had ever driven into, as he had to avoid the tree limbs. His steel troughs barely reached to the funnel. But it worked splendidly! The new concrete adhered nicely to the old foundation, and the combined thickness of the renewed foundation was in some places 18 inches! (Typical foundations for houses are 9 or 10 inches thick.) After the concrete dried, from inside the basement I filled in the six-inch wide gaps in the original foundation with hydro cement and hardware cloth. (Hardware cloth is woven wire mesh that is soldered at each joint.) We also installed drainage tile, covered by gravel, on the three sides of the house, and sloped the drainage to drywells. We have never had any significant flooding from the outside since completing this job. Now you know the kinds of things some teachers do with their spare time!

Have you ever cut down a tall tree? There are hidden dangers and problems in trying to be an instant forester! We had a dead maple tree that was about 38 feet tall and had a trunk about 26" in diameter. It was located only some five feet from the northwest corner of the house, so it needed to be taken down carefully, a section at a time. Deciding to do it myself, in the summer of 1987 I rented a 23" chainsaw weighing 30 pounds, and anchored 8" lag screws into the trunk for footholds. I tied a rope belt around my waist for "safety." Our two oldest children, Tim and Ruth, plus Carol and neighbor Alan each took turns holding a strong rope tied around the section of trunk I was cutting, so the trunk could be quickly pulled away from the house when it was cut free. I topped the tree first, and then made my way down the trunk, making the final cut about a yard above the ground. The next day I began cutting up the fallen tree into logs at 6:00 a.m. Soon, a sheriff appeared and said a neighbor had complained about the noise of the chain saw! So I rested that day and finished the job, beginning at 9:00 a.m. the third day. I wrote that every muscle in my body was sore and that, while cutting, I had drunk about a gallon of water and lemonade. On the first day, I put 11 hours into this tree-cutting project; on the third day, 12 hours. I remarked: "Everything in my body above my waist seems out of place. I moan and groan whenever I turn over in bed!" I got a chiropractor friend to put my vertebrae back into place. Professionals could have done this job much more efficiently and safely. But that would have cost us about $500, which we couldn't spare.

CHAPTER 4
TEACHER AS FAMILY MAN

A. Children

During the nine months prior to our first child's birth, Carol made a lot of preparation for his arrival. We had several baby showers. Carol did a great deal of sewing for maternity dresses, a receiving quilt, and other items. She gradually got used to the rather disruptive morning sickness. We bought and modified used furniture to place in Baby's bedroom.

Our first-born, Timothy, came to us on Sunday, June 25, 1967 at West Suburban Hospital, Oak Park, Illinois. I was scheduled to preach in Chicago, but because Carol was in labor, I asked my friend Al Classen to preach in my stead. He graciously consented on very short notice, and Carol and I have always been grateful! I wrote at the time, "Timothy looked vigorous, red, with dark hair and lots of it." Carol and I named him Timothy because, just as the Timothy in the Bible was the spiritual son of Paul, so our son was the physical son of Paul. We gave him the middle name Dwight after Dwight L. Moody. For the first six weeks, Timothy cried a lot and gained very little weight. We discovered that he was allergic to milk. We tried various formulas, and finally found one he could digest. When he was three weeks old, Dorothy Martin, wife of the Dean of Faculty, came to visit him and brought a gift. To our great embarrassment, Timothy burped out all his milk, tea, and cereal while Mrs. Martin held him, and thoroughly soiled her lovely dress!

When Timothy was about seven weeks old, we took him with us to a camping vacation in Peninsula State Park, Wisconsin. We tented next to our friends, the Al Classen family. In Ephraim, Wisconsin, we rented a leaky 16-foot boat. Because of a high cliff dropping down to the lake, there was no simple way to get Timothy into the boat, so we put him into a picnic basket, covered him with a table cloth, and lowered him into the boat from the cliff, using a long rope tied to the basket handle. We had to bail water from the boat during our entire ride, but Timothy was asleep in his basket, oblivious to the precarious situation he was in!

As Timothy grew, he became more and more fun to play with. I recorded in my diary when he learned to stick out his tongue, turn over, sit in a chair, when he got his first tooth, learned to crawl, to walk, when he first said "Da Da," when he began to wave at people, and when he uttered his first complete sentence!

In addition to housekeeping and caring for Tim, Carol attended an evening class twice a week at the newly established College of DuPage. I stayed home with Tim on those evenings. In my diary I described a difficult day Timothy had when he was seven months old: "Timothy had a bad day today. He pulled the kitchen TV table down on top of himself, including the heavy meat board on it; he pulled the record player off its stand and turned it over on the floor; and this evening he rolled off the bed where he was sitting, and bumped his head on the floor! He cried for about 45 minutes. I tried to comfort the poor fellow!"

When Tim was ten months old, I had him with me in my office one afternoon. I observed, "Timothy was a good boy, but he is a real bibliophile, insisting on taking books out of my library without signing them out!" Just before Tim's first birthday, Carol and I re-established family devotions as a regular daily activity. We included reading a Bible story to Tim, singing a children's hymn such as "Jesus Loves Me, This I Know," and prayer. We were also regular users of the Wheaton and West Chicago public libraries, and checked out about five children's books every two to three weeks. Children love repetition, and ours insisted we read these storybooks over and over. They often memorized whole books just from hearing them read to them and looking at the pictures.

During three weeks in July 1968, both Carol and I drove into Moody with Timothy so she could take a class. I wrote, "All the old maids who work in Crowell Hall (they are as the sand of the seashore for multitude) are learning of Timothy's 'attendance' at Arts and Crafts class, and he has a half-dozen visitors each day, besides others in Fitzwater Hall!"

Ruth Ann, our second child, was born July 8, 1969. I went to work after only two hours of sleep that day, and gave out "Baby Ruth" candy bars to my students! We "farmed out" Timothy to various friends while Carol was in the hospital. At six months, Ruth learned to laugh heartily at Tim's antics. She loved to be bounced. When Ruth was only eight months old she began to talk. I noted that she began to say "Da-Da-Da-Da" and kept it up incessantly!

After Ruth was born, Carol and I established what was to become a tradition in our home—a more extended playtime that we called Family Night. Once a week we took extra time to enjoy special activities with our children. We played longer games with them, and sometimes took them out to special activities and playgrounds, ate out with them, and did other activities that they enjoyed.

But we also played with our kids and spent time with them on almost a daily basis. I often played with the kids in the evening after supper. Carol played with them quite a lot during the day, and often joined me in playing with them in the evening as well. We called this "together time." Some of our favorite outdoor games were ghost midnight, tag, duck on the rock, and hide and seek. In ghost midnight, we all stood at a designated starting place in front of our neighbor's house at night. We had a countdown to 20, during which time each participant hid somewhere within "the boundaries" in the yard around the house. Then we yelled, "Ghost Midnight!" and the runner tried to find and tag the hidden children before they could run to safety around the house and leap into the starting place. The first one to be tagged became the next runner.

In duck on the rock, all the players lined up behind the sidewalk dividing the front lawn with a small rubber ball or tennis ball in hand. On a stump or upside down bucket some 20 or 25 feet away, the person who was "it" placed his ball under a can, then stood near it. Each person in turn threw his own ball at the can, trying to knock the can off the stump. If the thrower succeeded, the one who was "it" had to replace the ball and tag the thrower before he could run back to safety behind the sidewalk. If the thrower missed the can, he had to stand near his own ball where it landed. He would then watch for an opportunity to pick up the ball and run back to safety. If he was tagged while carrying the ball, the tagged person would then be "it."

When Tim was 2 1/2 we bought him a red wagon. We enjoyed giving Tim and Ruth, and later, Joy, rides in this wagon in our basement. Our basement was laid out like the Circus Maximus, with posts near each end. So we would pull the kids around the posts in the wagon. Every once in a while we would bump into a post as we rounded the curve, and dump the kids out on the floor. When we acquired two old tricycles, one child (usually Tim) would peddle his tricycle ahead of or behind the wagon in our "Circus Maximus" in the basement. We had loads of fun and frequent small accidents! We also had a swing suspended from the rafters in the basement (the basement had no wallboard at the time). The kids loved to swing in it, but the concrete floor was rough on them when they fell.

In nice weather we gave the children wagon rides on Barnes Avenue where we live. Barnes has a fairly steep slope down from our house to Sunset Avenue. Sometimes I would ride in the wagon, with one child between my legs. We would make a sharp turn to the right when we got to Sunset Avenue. This was especially important if we met a car coming down Sunset. Sometimes one child would be posted at the intersection to warn us of cross traffic. But these signals were not always clear, and we did have some near misses! I also had a basket over the rear wheel of my bike, and we would sometimes put a child in it and give him or her a bike ride in the basket.

One evening we "had a hilarious together time by making sock doll dresses." Another evening we made and put up a tent right on the living room floor. On still another evening we drew funny pictures and played musical chairs. We read books to them several evenings each week. A number of these together times were spent playing "dress up," where we donned the most outrageous costumes we could find and modeled them to everyone's delight. Other times were spent on potato races or charades. (A potato race had two pie plates containing three potatoes each at one end of the "race track.," and two empty pie plates at the other end. Each child had to pick up one potato and carry it to the opposite end and place it in a pie pan, then run back to retrieve the second or third potato. Whoever got the third potato into the pie pan first, won.)

Sometimes we made up fictitious stories on the spot, and had the children take turns doing the same. This was a good exercise for the imagination. We discovered that Carol has an outstanding talent for story telling. Some together times were spent in the public library in the children's section. When the kids were small, we began checking out several children's storybooks from the public library each week or two, and we read them over and over to our kids. They really looked forward to these opportunities to snuggle up in our laps and enjoy the pictures and text.

Our kids loved to watch "Sesame Street" on TV when they were little. Sometimes I would sing, "Five People in Our Family, one, two, three, four, five," applying it to the Nevin family. They also enjoyed "Mr. Roger's Neighborhood" many times. But we strictly limited our TV viewing and that of our kids. Our only TV set, which was black and white, was kept in the basement, half of which we later made into a recreation room. We felt that there were some special programs that were both entertaining and educational, but that most TV fare was shallow, stupid, and sometimes unwholesome. For quite a few years we enjoyed "How the Grinch Stole Christmas" and "Rudolph the Red-nosed Reindeer" at Christmastime. But we spent much more time playing interactive games and reading to the children than in watching TV. For a while we set up a tumbling mat in the recreation room, using an old mattress, pillows, and a love seat.

When the kids grew older, we played ball with them, had races, or took bike rides together (their little bikes by our big bikes). They also enjoyed the exercise bar and swing set we put in our back yard, and the sand box as well. Occasionally on a Saturday we visited museums, zoos, art galleries, or took a short trip (e.g., Starved Rock State Park, House on the Rock, Kettle Moraine). Sometimes we drove the family into Chicago and attended some sort of fun program like a puppet show or a drama, or went to a museum or exhibit. We attended some of the basketball games when they played on a school team, or a drama they were involved in, and we attended our share of circuses and fairs.

Our house in West Chicago was well suited for playing hide and seek, sometimes with all the lights out. One of the craziest things we did was to zip myself and each kid into a sleeping bag, with a pillow behind their necks for protection, then tumble down the thirteen stairs between the second and first floors. The kids thought it was hilarious! Amazingly, none of us ever got hurt in this activity!

One day in 1970 we had a visit from the Haley's, missionaries to Argentina, along with their five boys. We were tired, as we had just returned from a vacation to Canada. The Haley's were tired also, since they had been on the road in deputation. (Deputation is a term for missionaries' raising prayer and financial support through visiting churches, groups, and individuals, usually during furlough from their field of ministry. They now call it home assignment.) I wrote in my diary about the Haley family, "One of their excitable and very tired boys fell on the concrete basement stairs and cut his lip with his teeth. Tim fell out of his wagon, Ruthie fell out of her stroller, Stephen [Haley] ran over his foot with the wagon, and several other boys sustained lesser injuries. Jim [Haley] swallowed a moth while showing me a map of Argentina!" Quite a day!

When Tim was age 2 1/2, at my insistence, Carol began to require him to pick up his toys and put them in their correct places on the toy shelf in the living room before I came home. She drew little pictures to help him remember where they went. This lasted for a while, but eventually we both acknowledged that it was unrealistic. Later, the children were required to replace the toys anyplace on the toy shelf. But even this did not work very well. So I built a large toy box, and the kids would toss their toys into it for pickup time. That practice continued for many years. We still have the toy box, since I always built things to last! Come to think of it, we still have a buffet which I finished building in high school woodshop in 1950. It is over 50 years old, and still serves as a game cabinet.

Once in a while, Carol would take our kids with her to the Springfield, Illinois area for a few days to see her parents or siblings. I wrote in 1971 on one of these occasions, "I surely miss the family! Batching it is for the birds!" It was always wonderful to see my family again after they had been away!

When Ruth was almost 3, I wrote in my diary of a Sunday church service: "Ruthie went through a whole church service (and a long one at that) for the first time."

When Ruth was age 3 1/4, I noted that she often used an alibi such as "I have dust in my eyes" or "My tummy is hot!" when she didn't want to go to sleep after being put to bed.

For Timothy's fifth birthday, I built a very nice plywood tree house and attached it to a large limb on one of our maple trees. The other end of the tree house was supported by 4 x 4 posts. The tree house had a gable roof covered with roll roofing, and real transparent plastic windows that could be opened and closed. A "front porch" was outside the entry door, and I built a wooden rung ladder to access this porch. After it was totally finished, Tim and I slept one night in it. Tim enjoyed it, and I endured it (I had to sleep with my legs bent to fit inside). Our cat crawled up the ladder and visited us. Two days later, Ruth, 3, joined me in sleeping in the tree house.

Beginning in 1972, Tim entered kindergarten at Wheaton Christian Grammar School. After his first day, Tim said, "I learned too much today, Mommy!" Carol asked why, and he explained that it was because the teacher didn't leave enough time for the children to take their full nap! All three of our kids attended this same school through the eighth grade. It was a big financial struggle for us to pay tuition, but we believed that the Christian influences on our children and the commendable academic standards of this school made it all worthwhile. Each of our children later attended West Chicago Community High School, so they were not insulated from contact with non-Christian kids. Tim expressed this preference first, and the other children ultimately made the same decision. Wheaton Christian High School (today known as Wheaton Academy) was nearby, but the curriculum was limited, and the price was high. Tim also began the trend of the children attending West Chicago Bible Church while Mom and Dad stayed with Wheaton Bible Church. Quite a few of their friends from high school attended at the West Chicago church.

My family celebrated my fortieth birthday with a nice cake, decorated with the cartoon character "Snoopy," a gift of a "C" clamp from Ruthie (3 1/2), a hammer holder from Tim (5 1/2), and an indoor-outdoor thermometer from Carol. They made a paper crown and put it on my head as "King for a Day." But I was depressed the whole day, and nothing could cheer me. I felt that I was truly "over the hill" with no going back!

On August 14, 1972, we learned that Carol was pregnant with our third child. I wrote: "The Lord slipped this one over on us; we really weren't planning on a third child—but we're thrilled anyway. If that's what the Lord wants, it's what we want too! Carol celebrated by buying a string of lollypops!" We gave the tentative name of Daniel Ashby Nevin to our third child, thinking it would surely be a boy. But the Lord had a surprise for us.

On March 4, 1973, Joy Elizabeth Nevin was born. We had the same obstetrician deliver each child (Dr. Skiles) at the same hospital (West Suburban Hospital, Oak Park). Dr. Skiles had denied me access to see the first two children born, so I expressed a strong desire to watch the birth of our third. He grudgingly permitted me into the delivery room after I donned paper trousers, paper shoes, and paper hat. What a thrill and privilege to see a new little life come into the world!

Two weeks later, I bottle-fed and changed Joy all by myself. It took me a whole hour, as I was out of practice! A week later, I was able to do this in 30 minutes. We hired a young lady from our church for a week to help us with caring for Carol, Joy, and the other kids and to do some of the housework. That was a great relief to Carol and me, and enabled Carol to regain her strength more quickly.

When Joy was 3 1/2 months old, she laughed at me twice! This was the first time she'd ever laughed, and I thought it an honor to be laughed at by our baby daughter!

When Timothy was nearly 6, I declared "Timothy Day" in my classes and told four Timothy stories before giving final exams to the students. They enjoyed the stories and were better able to relax while they took their exams. When Tim was almost 6, "my relationship with him made real strides when I admitted that I had the same problem I thought he had—that of forgetting what we were supposed to be doing" by getting off the track through musing on abstract topics. For his sixth birthday, we gave Tim a new children's bike and a tetherball. I gave rides in our new steel wheelbarrow to the six kids who attended his birthday party.

When Tim was 6 and Ruth was 4, I wrote, "Timothy has been doing <u>marvelously</u> in his swimming lessons this week! Ruthie has learned to put her head under the water." As the kids grew old enough, I used to wrestle with them on the living room carpet. Sometimes I would be "attacked" by all three at one time! This was a lot of fun, but eventually the three of them got too powerful for old dad, and I had to quit the practice.

By age 6 Tim had memorized the names of all the known types of dinosaurs. He became a child expert on these ancient critters! He went trick-or-treating with Carol on Halloween, and dressed in a homemade stegosaurus dinosaur costume. Ruth was dressed as a European princess. Carol gave cupcakes and a personal evangelistic tract as they went door to door.

At age 6, Tim got all excited about selling "doggie rides" and tunes on the flute and harmonica to raise money from his friends. He also wanted to run off ads to let others know of his services. The goal? To purchase a non-existent, bellows type mini-bike! A few days later, Tim put on two puppet shows, charging three cents for each performance.

While our children were still small, we read C. S. Lewis' *Narnia Tales* to them. They loved the whole series. Lewis became important to me, too, as I read many of his works, both fiction and non-fiction.

When Joy was 6 months old, we brought our entire family to Moody Church's Camp Moyoca, where I was the principle speaker for the 3-day Labor Day weekend. Almost all of the young adults at the camp held Joy at one time or another. I remarked about Joy at 6 months: "Joy is drinking from a glass now . . . She really loves to eat! She's also <u>very</u> alert. Praise the Lord for such fine children!" When Joy was almost 1 year old, I babysat with the three kids all day Saturday while Carol gave an address at a women's meeting. Joy tumbled down the front stairs in her walker and bumped her head! I am very grateful that children can survive so many bumps!

When Joy was 1 year old, she began to greet me with "Hi, Dad!" At 15 months, she was walking quite well, but still crawled much of the time. At 1 1/2, Joy was "very active, jumping around, clowning off and getting into everything."

We had more than our share of sickness. The week before Easter, 1974, I was sick for a week. Then Carol and Joy took sick, then Tim and Ruth got sick, each being under the weather for several days. It was the worst siege of illness our family had ever been through! Tim and Ruth went to the doctor, and only <u>Ruth</u> got the shot. She felt utterly betrayed!

When Tim turned 7, he was up at 5:30 a.m., running about the house and singing "Happy Birthday to me," alternated by the inflating of balloons. I had never seen him so excited! We had a nice party with eight of his friends. About this time we purchased a vinyl wading pool, ten feet across and two feet deep. The kids loved it.

During the years our kids were in grade school, no bus service was available. So we formed car pools with other student's parents. Carol would make the morning run and later, the afternoon run, and do errands in between squeezing in what housework she could. For 19 years we had three school kids but only one car. Although this was doable, it was quite a hassle, since Carol had to take one child at a time to his or her particular function. I often told Carol that, should necessity require it, she would make a splendid cabbie! She knew all the roads in our section of DuPage County, and the short cuts to getting almost anywhere! When our one car broke down, we were really in a bind, and were forced to depend upon friends and neighbors for temporary transportation.

One of our family policies was "beginner plates." The child had to eat at least a teaspoonful of each food on his first plate. This included vegetables. The least favorite foods for the kids were peas and celery. Sometimes peas were secretly fed to the dog, who was often under the dinner table to receive any fallout or free handouts available! Most of the time, our dog wouldn't eat peas either! Some peas were smashed and concealed inside a napkin. It is debatable whether beginner plates could be considered a success to insure a balanced diet, since they sometimes caused resentment. Our kids, now adults, still don't like peas! (Tim makes an exception for peas in Indian curries.) But each of our adult children eats veggies and salad today. One is even a vegetarian! So I take it that beginner plates were not a total failure.

Where there are children, pets are sure to follow. Besides Oliver, the dog, we had many different pets while our children were growing up, including Noah the goldfish, Nathaniel the cat, Smoky the cat, various small fish that Ruth kept, Piggy the guinea pig, a salamander, numerous hamsters, a rabbit or two, Snoopy the dog, Pooki the cat, who had a love-hate relationship with Snoopy, and eventually became so friendly with the dog that he slept with her. The dog was a Jack Russell type terrier. Tim had a parakeet named Tazoo, but it died from sleeping in a draft. Tazoo was replaced with Dynamite, a hamster. Snoopy the dog was succeeded by Ziggy, (a full-blooded beagle), a short-lived hermit crab who was fed peanut butter and stayed in his sea shell house so much we hardly ever saw him, white mice, and who knows what else? At one point (1974) we had one tiny goldfish for each family member! In the summer of 1982 Carol took Ruth, 11, to Detroit to pick up a 9-week old golden retriever puppy, to be raised for a leader dog for the blind. Ruth named her puppy "Teddy," and we all loved the dog. Ruth spent many hours training it to heel and taking it everywhere a leader dog would need to go. Unfortunately, due to a hip dysplasia, Teddy did not make the grade as a leader dog, but he did get a good home when he was returned to Detroit a year or two later. Ruth was very sad to part with her dog!

When Joy was 2 we had a lovely birthday party for her, and invited a neighbor family to join us. But apparently the party lasted too long, since Joy fell asleep before we could cut the decorated cake!

Tim, at 8, wrote a fictitious story, complete with drawing, of a dog tearing off our pastor's trousers. I shared the story with my classes, and they roared with laughter! Also at 8, Tim had his first piano recital. I also wrote in my 1976 diary "I sat with Tim while he practiced piano with much complaining and tears!" Taking piano lessons was a pain for Tim and for his mother as well, who had to suffer through his practice sessions. But Tim's teacher admonished him, "Don't ever quit." He did persevere for some time after that, but finally, we released him from this obligation, as it was not worth the hassle.

When Tim was 8 and 9, he enjoyed attending Awana. (Awana is a Christian children's club that emphasizes Scripture memory and competitive games.) Once for Awana, Tim dressed as a hobo, and they served hobo stew! This stew was made from unlabeled food cans brought by all the boys, and their contents were dumped together into the same large pot. Rumor had it that someone had brought dog food. The whole mess was cooked and served!

In 1975, we were influenced by reading James Dobson's *Dare to Discipline*. And so we started to use Dobson's positive reinforcement award system by making a job list for our kids, with their daily and Saturday work assignments posted on a wall chart. We rewarded them with a penny for each job completed. (Most jobs were tiny ones.) For Joy, who was only 2 1/2 at the time, we substituted candy for pennies. We upped the ante by making longer jobs worth more. This system functioned fairly well for several years. But sometimes I hassled the kids to get their Saturday jobs done. This became a drag on our family life. Finally, in 1986, I changed my managerial style from harassment to deadlines with penalties for deadlines missed. The kids could go at any pace they liked so long as they met their deadlines. This proved to be much more pleasant for everyone, as well as more effective.

It was a family custom for quite a few years to invite two or three other couples, personal friends from our church, out to our house on July 4th for a picnic and outdoor and indoor games. We invited the Tahls, the Schoenthals, and the Thorns.

Carol often brought our kids to Moody so she could attend the Faculty Wives' Fellowship, or to show them off to the students and employees. She established a tradition of bringing them all into Moody at least once a semester, on a day when our children's school was closed. They would bring a few toys with them, and Carol and our children would take about 10 minutes in each of my classes for a "show and tell" session. As late as 1980 Carol and our three kids visited all three of my classes and had lots of fun. Joy at age 7 showed her Snoopy stuffed dog and walking doll; Ruth at age 11 showed her mitten puppets and super balls; and Tim who was 13 showed his stamps. This was a total delight to the students, and the kids were often highly entertaining. Carol would interview each child in front of the students, and then have them demonstrate some toy or trick they had brought with them. When they were really small, she would stand them on the teacher's table so all the students could see them. Each child would exhibit a favorite toy. Sometimes during their visit, Joy would sneak behind me and draw a caricature of their Daddy's face on the chalkboard for all the students to enjoy!

Three sets of books that our kids loved and used frequently after they learned to read were *The Family Bible Library*, by V. Gilbert Beers (10 volumes); *Childcraft* (15 volumes); and *The Illustrated Encyclopedia of the Animal Kingdom* (12 volumes). We read to them from these books and hundreds more before they could read for themselves. Another favorite was *The Bible in Pictures for Little Eyes*, by Kenneth Taylor. We were thrilled when this book was put on a set of recordings with the narration done by Bill Pearce. Our children listened to the records for hours on end. When Ruth was 4, she listened to all 16 of the records narrating 182 Bible stories, without stopping, while following along in the book. I was amazed!

Each year in October, the whole family would join in raking our leaves into a huge pile under our Norway maple tree (our favorite climbing tree). The children would then jump into the leaf pile from a stepladder or a low branch. It was hard on allergies but lots of fun!

While Carol did most of the nurturing and caring for our kids, I did help with them a lot. Many times I played with them, read stories to them, and put them to bed in the evening when Carol was tired or had other appointments.

In 1977 we instituted what we called the Family Conference Table for our children and ourselves. In this forum, we would exchange ideas with one another, make plans, voice complaints, and work on solutions in a quasi-democratic fashion.

Several times our family went to the Rollerama (a roller rink) in Lombard. I tried once to learn to skate while at the Rollerama. I carried a pillow under my bottom, and clung tightly to the handrail. Carol held me while I wobbled all over. But it was no use. The family had a lot of fun watching my agony!

When Joy was age 4, we made a tape of her singing the Gaither's popular children's song, "I'm a Promise, I'm a Possibility." I played it for my classes. They thought it was a scream! That year also, Joy was the flower girl for the wedding of a Moody student couple we knew. Unfortunately, she fell off of our deck and broke her arm just before the wedding. So she performed her flower girl duties in a beautiful peach colored dress with white apron, white shoes, and a white arm cast and lace and sling that Carol made! Ruth also walked off the deck backwards a different time and hit her head, so I finally installed a rope guardrail around the deck's edges.

Tim has always had quite a sense of humor. He began laughing even before he could talk! When he was 10, one of our friends was serving the punch at a farewell party for a church couple who were moving away. Tim brought his paper cup and held it over the punch bowl for a refill. Pat kept dipping and filling the cup, but it never became full. (Tim had punched holes in the bottom of the cup!)

In July 1977, we packed up the family, tents, and other supplies in our station wagon and drove out to California for what turned out to be a memorable vacation. Tim was 10, Ruth was 8, and Joy was 4. Our intinerary included two stops at Carol's parents' farm in Central Illinois, and visits with many of her relatives. We explored Meramec Caverns in Missouri. The kids roller-skated at rest stops; we had frequent motel stays, and visited colorful restaurants and museums. We saw a rodeo in Santa Fe, New Mexico; camped in our tent in the mountains of the Santa Fe National Forest; visited with missionary friends in Thoreau, New Mexico; and saw the Painted Desert and Petrified Forest in Arizona. Our California stay included a tour of my boyhood houses and haunts in the towns of San Dimas, La Verne, Pomona, Charter Oak, and Covina. We had the use of a Moody grad, Steve Holz's, apartment in Fullerton for about a week. Steve Holz had been a student of mine at Moody, where I had spent many hours counseling him. He now had a lovely wife and two kids. He treated each member of our family to rides in a 2-seater single-motor Cessna, since he was working for Mission Aviation Fellowship as a missionary pilot. The Holz family then went on vacation while we occupied their apartment with a swimming pool nearby. We visited Disneyland and Marineland of the Pacific. We saw my relatives, including two of my brothers and Carol's mother. We also visited with friends at BIOLA and Talbot Theological Seminary, a grad of Pacific Bible College, and Moody grads. We enjoyed a surprise homecoming visit with the president and some of my former students at The Los Angeles Bible Training School. We also spent time with friends at the Church of the Open Door,

Los Angeles. On the way back we stopped in Utah at the Dinosaur National Monument. We stayed with Moody grads Jim and Ruth Olson in their knotty pine ranch house at Pagosa Springs, Colorado. We visited with my relatives in Mc Pherson, Kansas, went to a zoo in Garden City, and stayed with friends near Kansas City. We arrived back home in Illinois after 25 days, 6,200 miles, and all on a budget of $820.00!

But the next day we all showed the wear and tear of our journey. I noted in my dairy: "Ruth and Joy each had fevers last night and yesterday. Tim developed one today. Ruth broke a thermometer yesterday, and Carol one today! Carol broke a plate today, and I lost my car in the parking lot."

When our family visited Moody, Tim loved to see the radio studios of WMBI. He developed quite an interest in radio broadcasting, which was later to show up in his producing and hosting a weekly international music program for the University of Illinois, Chicago's campus station, WUIC-Flames Radio.

In late winter, early 1978, the kids put on a ragtime band concert for an audience of two! Our kids also put on a "children's zoo" in 1978. The animals were a nest of field mice that Tim and Ruth found!

In 1978 I played touch football on a wet lawn with Tim and two neighbor kids, Randy and Dean. My knee buckled underneath me while I tackled Dean, and it was very painful. I spent several days in the hospital, but they decided I would not need surgery—just a cast for five weeks. I quickly learned to walk in my cast with or without crutches.

When Tim was 11 and Ruth was 9, Carol took them to see the original animated version of the film, *The Fellowship of the Ring,* based on J. R. R. Tolkein's Trilogy, *Lord of the Rings.* Ruth tossed and turned that night, but did get to sleep eventually. Tim couldn't sleep because of the horrifying scene when the ring-wraiths attempted to assassinate Frodo and company, so he brought his sleeping bag into our bedroom at 1:00 a.m., and then was able to sleep. Some three years later, Tim, Ruth and I discussed *The Fellowship of the Ring* and Joy, who was almost over her nighttime fears, again became afraid. So it was a holy terror getting her to sleep."

In February 1979, our family drove to fellow faculty member David Smart's house in Skokie, Illinois and enjoyed their snow slide. From an eight-foot elevation, you slid down in a saucer, then up the side of an embankment, and around the garage to the alley in back! A neat experience!

In the fall of 1978, my neighbor, Phil Warsop, excavated under his house to put in a basement. But rain and snow eroded the dirt foundation the house rested on, and nearly caused his house to collapse into his basement excavation! So the Warsops stayed with us for ten days in the spring of 1979 until Phil made enough repairs to stabilize his house. Randy, Phil's son was close to Tim's age. The night before April 1 (April Fool's Day) they stayed up until 1:30 a.m., dreaming and scheming! They put sugar in the saltshaker, put a frog in the bathtub, a centipede in the washbasin, and pulled other tricks on all of us.

For several years, Tim and Ruth and Joy went to 4-H meetings. This farm organization provided an outlet for their creativity. Joy even showed rabbits at the DuPage County Fair. All our children participated in various clubs, and at church, Pioneer Girls and Awana.

I spent lots of time playing ping-pong, Frisbee, catch, and going on bike rides with Tim. Later, we did the same with Ruth and Joy.

When Tim was 12, he and I joined a group of about 30 dads and lads and went caving at Buckner's Cave near Bloomington, Indiana. There were some very tight places in the cave as we crawled around on our stomachs. We were equipped with hard hats, flashlights, and canteens of water. A couple of dads were overcome by claustrophobia early in the tour, and backed out. Another, a heavier dad, got stuck in "the Corkscrew," a narrow vertical passage that we had to wiggle through by twisting our bodies at the right places and times. But all in all we had a good day of it. Tim and I loved it!

Tim, at age 12, planned to do a skit by playing John the Baptist with his head in a platter! Carol rigged him up with a big carton, and then Tim knelt under the carton and stuck his head out the top through a real platter!

Tim first developed an interest in stamp collecting when he was 9 years old. By the time he was 12, he became an avid international stamp collector, and began attending the Philatelic Society in Glen Ellyn, Illinois. Eventually he specialized in the British Caribbean colonies, and developed an excellent collection, especially stamps from St. Lucia.

When Tim was age 13, he and I spent quite a few hours together building a plant-watering machine for his school science project. We called it "the Green Machine." A toy car equipped with a dart traveled down a rotary track like a roller coaster, pricked an inflated balloon, and this released a lever that tipped a cup of water, which in turn watered a potted flower! And it even worked for the science demonstration, to our mutual relief! I took half of the machine to Moody one day and half the next, and then demonstrated it in class. It worked the second or third try for each class.

When Joy was 8 we went for a vacation to the farm of a former Moody student couple, the Samples, in Cordova, IL, next to the Mississippi River. We had a wonderful time riding their pony, petting their cows, and watching their chickens. Joy waded off the riverbank, and cut her foot badly on an exposed clamshell. Joy had to make three visits to the doctor.

Tim loved April 1 (April Fool's Day). For April 1, 1982, I wrote in my diary: "I got up at 5:45 and discovered our favorite practical joker, Tim, had been at work. The bathroom wastebasket fell on my head and my fingers stuck to the toilet flush handle. By then I was alert enough to look for other possibilities, and I was not disappointed. He had mixed salt with the sugar, loosened the salt and peppershaker tops, and put glue on the refrigerator door and the hot and cold-water faucet handles. He arranged for the scissors to drop when I opened the refrigerator door. He put fake blood and hair and toads in the bathroom sink, "dead fish" in the cupboard, "blood" stains in the bathtub, and shaving cream on the toilet paper. I think he was awake and listening, but I said nothing. He hid my books under the sofa and substituted a heavy encyclopedia in my brief case. He also pulled the plugs from the radio and the toaster. The toast took a very long time! Carol's fingers were stuck on the toilet flush handle and refrigerator handle, then buttered up by the telephone.

Several summers the whole family and I enjoyed free films in the open air at Blackwell Forest Preserve in Warrenville, Illinois. The films featured nature and astronomy, mostly documentaries. The environment featured mosquitoes! We spent many happy hours at Blackwell.

Two of the kid's favorite fun places were Great America in Gurnee, Illinois and the Indiana Dunes. They went to both on quite a few occasions, mostly in the summer. Great America featured scary roller coasters and the Dunes were good places to play Frisbee, ball, and get some sun. They were near enough to Lake Michigan so they could swim as well.

Tim did a lot of biking during his teen years for exercise and enjoyment. He rode as much as forty or more miles in a day.

Our kids enjoyed their share of going to camp also. In June 1982, Joy went to Camp Timberlee (Wisconsin), Ruth to Bible Memory Association at Camp Michawana (Michigan), and Tim went on a Project Serve trip to Mendenhall, Mississippi with the Wheaton Bible Church youth group.

Joy at 9 took up typing. She typed this note to me:

DEAR DADDY WORK HARD & HOPE IT WONT RAINN! IL LIKE TY PING ! KEEP WORKING!

****

LOVE YOUR DAUTER ************* JOY

One summer morning the digging job around the house foundation was too much for Tim. Our friend Wayne Braun had come to work on the ditch, and Tim got up early to help him dig with a pickaxe. Carol and I were at a Faculty Retreat. We had a real scare when a friend called and told us Tim had passed out while working on the ditch, and was in Central DuPage Hospital! When we got there, he was partly alert, but barely coherent. He was exhausted. I stayed with him an hour or two, and Carol stayed with him the rest of the day. I saw him again that evening. They gave him a complete battery of tests. The doctor said he had had a seizure, but they didn't know what caused it. By the next day, Tim was pretty much back to normal. Strangely, he has never had a seizure before or since. We decided to close down the trench project for the season just before Thanksgiving, 1982. So we ordered 105 bales of straw to insulate the trenches during the winter. Besides filling the trenches with straw, the kids made a straw house with an umbrella "skylight" and three or four tunnels. Great fun!

That same semester, Carol, Ruth, and Joy came to class on Veteran's Day when public school was out. Ruth showed the students her photo album, talked of her dog, Teddy, and showed her mazes. Joy played "Mary Had a Little Lamb" on her flute, and had her wind-up ladybug crawl across the overhead projector. Carol talked about her studies at Wheaton Graduate School. (Tim was gone to an all-day high school event in West Chicago.)

By 1983 we began what became a family tradition: Carol and I took each of our kids, one at a time, to a Christmas dinner at a restaurant of their choice. We wanted to give each of our children a sense of personal importance by showing each one that we valued him or her as a separate person.

In 1985, after caring for our children for 18 years, loving them, feeding them, disciplining them, seeing to their education, transporting them to many activities, and being their friend and confidante, Carol remarked, "Parenting is the hardest thing I do." I noted in my diary that the same was true for me. But we could have added that parenting was also the most important thing that we did! We did enjoy many creative activities with our kids!

Tim graduated from high school in 1985. In the summer of 1986, when Tim was 19, we asked him to begin making his own way in the world. He requested a going away party, and we consented. We asked him to invite about 30 young people. But Tim had many friends in Chicago, and he lost track of how many he had invited. About 100 young people showed up! We asked our friend, Wayne Braun, to chaperone the party, and he did a great job, with no problems. A few of Tim's friends brought drums and band instruments, and they had a good time. Ruth attended the party, while Carol and Joy went to a friend's house until 1:30 a.m. and then returned home. I chickened out, and slept at Moody that night! I wrote Tim a going away letter. We saw Tim off as he left home the next day, bound for Madison, Wisconsin. This was to be a very significant event for all our family.

Ruth at 17 participated in a Christmas drama at church as an angel, and Carol and I went to see the play. I remarked to my diary, "She isn't one [angel] every day, you know!"

We had a surprise birthday party for Joy when she turned 15. Carol, Ruth, and Ruth's friend Jenny called a lot of Joy's friends to come to Pal Joey's for a pizza party. We expected about 30 to show up, but 55 kids packed the reserved room! Ruth brought Joy into a room filled with her friends, and it was a total shock to her. She was thrilled!

B. Tim at Moody

Tim was on his own beginning with the summer of 1986. After failing to find a job in Madison, Wisconsin, he walked 15 miles out of town to Lake Waubesa Bible Camp to ask for a counselor's job. One of the counselors had dropped out, so they decided to hire him. But they could not pay him; they gave him room and board only. After the camp was over, and fall was approaching, Tim suggested to us that he would like to attend Moody Bible Institute. Carol and I were thrilled that Tim wanted to go to Moody. We had to pay for his board and room, but were grateful that donors made it possible to provide a tuition-free education. Tim was not well impressed with some of the dorm rules and dress code, but he did make some great friends during his one year at Moody. In fact, some of these friends are still good buddies even today!

The first semester (fall, 1986) Tim attended classes rather faithfully, and studied some. But the second semester Tim was at Moody, his attendance became scattered and he studied very little. He did have a great time with his friends, though! He was on academic probation, and after one year, he was not permitted to continue. We talked about his Moody experience in 2004, and he affirms that it was a year when some very positive things happened. He learned much about himself and what he wanted to do in life and what he did not want to do. During his year at MBI, I often visited with him in my office, or had a snack with him in the Coffee Cove, or ate with him in the Cafeteria. We went out together occasionally, to an ethnic restaurant, a used bookstore, or a museum.

After his Moody experience, Tim attended a community college and brought his grades up. He worked as a bike messenger in Chicago, Washington, D.C., New York City, and San Francisco. Tim loves travel filled with adventure. He traveled to Mexico, various countries of Central America, and from there to Medellin, Colombia, where he visited my brother, Frank. He made straight A's at Austin Community College in Texas. Then Tim enrolled at the University of Illinois, Chicago, and earned a B.A. in history, followed by an M.A. in African history. While enrolled at UIC, Tim worked part-time as a taxicab driver in Chicago. Then he traveled to Nigeria, where he set up a small power radio station. He visited his sister, Ruth, in Spain, passed through Gibralter, and worked his way down through North Africa to Senegal and the Gambia. Tim lived in Ghana for a year and a half while employed by Overseas Processing Entity (a part of Church World Service). He did prelimi- nary interviewing of refugees from Liberia and Ivory Coast for possible relocation in the United States. He visited all but one of the countries of West Africa, followed by tours of South Africa and East Africa, for a total of 21 African countries. From there Tim visited in India, Thailand, Australia, and Taiwan before flying back to California. He is the first of our family to travel clear around the world! Tim just completed his third semester for a doctorate in African history at the University of Florida, Gainesville. In 2004 he married a Liberian, Zakpa Debra Paye, whom he met while living in Ghana.

C. Ruth at Moody

Our daughter Ruth loves horses. When she was 14, Carol took her out frequently to Danada Horse Stables, on the south side of Wheaton. It was a farm formerly owned by Dan and Ada Rice, hence the combined name, Danada. The horses and property came into the possession of the DuPage County Forest Preserve District. They welcomed volunteers to help care for the horses, and offered free riding lessons in exchange. Ruth volunteered at Danada, took riding lessons and quickly fell in love with the horses; so much so that she took her B.S. in Equine Science from Otterbein College near Columbus, Ohio.

But Ruth also loved her Savior and wanted to enter some kind of Christian service. This desire attracted her to Moody Graduate School. She attended three semesters, from January 1993 through May, 1994. She thoroughly enjoyed her studies there, her teachers, and the atmosphere of fellowship and camaraderie. Ruth was a commuter student, as she was living at home. She made some wonderful friends, some of whom she still keeps in touch with. Ruth continued at Moody Graduate School a year and a half, until marriage and missionary deputation interrupted her studies. Today, she serves with her husband, Jorge Torres, in the northeastern section of Spain under Greater Europe Mission. They met while Ruth was on a Wheaton Bible Church missions trip to Camp L'Arcada, in Spain. She has had some influence on the horse-riding program at Camp L'Arcada, near Banyoles, about two hours north of Barcelona. She still hopes to be involved with horses when their three children are old enough. She was given a pony by a fellow missionary, and the children are learning to ride it. Ruth and Jorge have now transitioned into working with the local evangelical church in Banyoles and the church plants in Salt and Blane. Ruth is providing leadership in the nursery and Sunday school, while Jorge is specializing in youth ministry, follow-up, discipleship, and designing websites.

Ruth and Jorge are the parents of Judah, Lucas, and Chantel. Their fourth child, whom they named Chloe Emma, was stillborn on August 3, 2004. Carol was there ten days before the expected birth, and then returned to Spain for five more days to comfort the grieving parents. Chloe was healthy right up to the end of her full term, but died in labor when Ruth's uterus ruptured at an old incision from her caesarean section five years earlier. We trust God will use this tragedy for his glory!

D. Joy's Love for Languages

Because Joy loved her study of French in junior high and high school and did so well with it, she chose The University of Illinois at Champaign/Urbana to earn a B.A. in French. While at the University of Illinois, Joy roomed with a Moody graduate, and they had good fellowship.

Joy quickly became so fluent in French that when she visited France, the French would not believe she was an American! God gave Joy a brilliant mind and a real talent with languages. She formally studied Spanish only two years, but was able to teach Spanish to middle school students quite well. Joy studied a year at the University of Strasbourg to further her French language and culture training. While living in France, Joy drove to Romania to attend the wedding of two of my former students, Cristian Barbosu and his fiancée, Anne. Joy later earned a master's degree in French from the University of California at Santa Barbara in three successive summers. The pleasant weather and the nearby beaches were not hard to take either! In 1996 Joy married a fine Christian man, Knute Axelson, and taught French seven years in private schools before their first child, Soren Gustaf, was born in 2003. They are active in their church and in home Bible studies. Joy is also a volunteer with World Relief and teaches ESL (English as a Second Language) to a French-speaking refugee family from Burundi.

And so, my relation to Moody Bible Institute has not only been my major contribution to God's Kingdom, but it has impacted the lives of each of our children as well. Nor will I ever cease to be grateful that God led me to marry a Moody student!

CHAPTER 5

MY EXPERIENCES AS A CLASSROOM TEACHER

A. Classroom Experiences

In my second semester of teaching, I was assigned a class in biblical hermeneutics (how to interpret the Bible). Soon I was called into the dean of faculty's office and was told that one of my students complained that I didn't seem to know where I was going in this course. He was probably right, but I assured the dean that I would get it better organized. I was actually trying to teach hermeneutics and Bible study methods in a two-hour course, and the content was overcrowded. One of my students left an apple and a note on my desk. The note read, "How about skipping the mid-term exam?" I demurred and told the class later, "The apple wasn't big enough!"

The final exam in my first hermeneutics class was a real hair-pulling event! It contained 100 tough multiple-choice questions, filled with double negatives that completely confused the students. Students kept coming to my desk, asking me to explain the questions. But soon after, my skills as a test writer improved, and I learned to produce exams that were fair, tested the students on what they had studied, and covered the entire unit or course in a balanced manner, avoiding trivia questions.

Hermeneutics and Bible study methods were later to become two of my specialties, and I thoroughly enjoyed teaching them.

Quizzes assessed how students were doing week by week. Some were announced; others were known as pop quizzes, because they were given unannounced. Students dreaded pop quizzes, especially if they were behind in their studies (a not uncommon experience). One of my colleagues was so well known for his pop quizzes that someone made him a leather pouch to carry the 4x6 quiz pad on his belt. That way he was prepared to give a pop quiz at any time! After a few years, I discontinued pop quizzes, knowing that they generated resentment and increased the stress of learning.

One day I headed for my next class to teach hermeneutics, a bit behind schedule. When I got there, I found that the students had turned out the lights, turned on a movie projector set up for another class, and proceeded to watch the movie. I was thoroughly confused, thinking I had come to the wrong classroom! When I finally realized it was my own class, we all had a good laugh!

In January 1970, we were evacuated from a second floor classroom in Fitzwater Hall because a pipe burst and flooded the room. So we moved to a classroom on the first floor, only to find that we had a waterfall in half of the room because of the broken pipe above us! We moved the piano out of the classroom, had the students sit in the dry part of the room, while I kept on teaching.

About once or twice a month, visitors from out of town would sit in on my classes. Some of these were friends of mine, and others, strangers. But they usually said afterwards that they enjoyed the classes a great deal.

During two or three different semesters, my Prison and Pastoral Epistles class put on a drama featuring Onesimus, the runaway slave in the book of Philemon who heard the gospel in Rome where he had met the Apostle Paul in a Roman prison. I would invite other faculty members and classes to attend. My students really put their best efforts into these plays, and they made me proud of their acting! The script was always written by a student in the class, based on the text of Philemon.

In the early years, one of my responsibilities was to teach one or two classes each year to the Married Women's Guild. These women were married to Day School students, and many of them had children. As a novice teacher and workaholic, I greatly overestimated how much homework the women could handle. I tended to overload them with assignments, and some of them dropped out; others complained. One day I left campus early to look at a house for rent.

The next day I was told that everyone was looking for me on the previous afternoon, as I was supposed to give an exam to the Guild ladies. I had completely forgotten it, but the lady in charge of the Married Women's Guild found the master copy of the exam and dictated it to the class. She was quoted as saying, "He ought to have every hair pulled out of his head," but the fact was that I didn't have any hair to spare! I did apologize to the class and to several administrators for this unfortunate incident.

Another time in the Undergraduate Division (we called it Day School at that time) I got so absorbed in reading the newspaper in my office that I forgot to go to my theology class. At twenty minutes after the class began, several students came to my office to inform me that I had forgotten to go to class. (Students were permitted to leave class if the professor was more than ten minutes late.) "We have a suggestion," they announced. "We think you should save your cuts till the end of the semester!" I really felt foolish.

A few times, my students complained that I seldom smiled. I would explain in class, "I may not look like I smile very much, but I'm smiling inside." This was really true. I had little to smile about in my childhood and youth, and so I never developed a frequent smile in my facial expressions. But as I have grown older, I have learned to smile more often. When you are aware that God is your best friend, there is much to smile about, if you remember to do it!

In December 1973, I experienced an unusual movement of the Holy Spirit in my own life, a kind of personal revival. This began about December 10, and inevitably spread to my classes. I wrote a lengthy report of my emotions in my diary entry of December 13: "This morning I was so broken and tender in heart that I couldn't bring the regular lesson in Systematic Theology 305-1 (8:00 a.m.). I just shared with the class the tremendous burden on my heart for them, for their spiritual welfare, lovingly but pointedly admonishing them about possible personal sins, the need for restitution, the problem of discouragement, hypocrisy, defeat, selfish inconsiderateness, etc. I broke down and wept before them, prayed for them in love, and sat down. Johnny Washington, a student, prayed aloud and led us in "Spirit of the Living God." Students all over the class wept and prayed silently. God is at work. I asked any who felt led to do so to lead in prayer for the last eight minutes of class, and there were four or five who led in beautiful prayers. . . ."

Later that day, fifty high school students visited MBI on a field trip. They came to my class where I was showing a film on the occult, so we changed to a larger classroom that could accommodate them and my regular students as well in a course that I pioneered and taught, called Modern Religious Movements. After class, I invited our own students to talk with the high school students, and some of them did so, giving impressive testimonies to the reality of Jesus Christ in their lives. Two days later, I wrote: "So mightily has God worked in my life this week that I have been <u>forced</u> to lay aside <u>everything</u> else but a minimum of necessary business except for classes Monday through Thursday."

In 1977, in Systematic Theology, I was expounding on Tozer's *Pursuit of God* and had just explained his chapter on "The Blessedness of Possessing Nothing." Evidently the Lord took me seriously, for right after that I learned from Carol that we would be socked for about $850.00 for a new well pump, pipe, parts, and labor! I hurried to Bell Savings and Loan and wiped out all our savings to pay for this financial disaster. I then had the opportunity of meditating on "the blessedness of possessing nothing"!

Carol will testify that I have never been good at buying clothes that matched or were even close to being fashionable! My first consideration was cost, and so I brought home some very questionable "bargains." For example, one time I bought a brownish-orange wool tweed suit sprinkled with multi-colored threads that Carol loathed. I also bought a leisure suit that was a bright lime green, and even attended a wedding at the very sophisticated Fourth Presbyterian Church in it! Among the other fashion disasters was an orange leisure suit that I called my "pumpkin suit." Unfortunately, I was stubborn and unwilling to discard any of these threads until they were totally worn out. (I grew up in the "waste not, want not" school of the Great Depression!) Of course, I wore all of these to class many times. I suspect my students were greatly relieved when I finally came to class in more professional garb!

I always strove to make my courses practical. One assignment that I gave to students taking my systematic theology courses was to interview thirty people about how they would describe God or

Jesus Christ. Each year our students reported leading a number of interviewees to faith in Christ as a result of these assignments.

In 1981, in one of my systematic theology classes, a student played the most elaborate and amusing trick on me of my whole teaching career at Moody. While I was lecturing, a voice came over the public address system: "Dr. Nevin, this is American Airlines. Please pick up the nearest courtesy phone." Since my class was in Crowell Hall, I went to the Crowell Hall reception desk and asked if American Airlines had placed a call. They knew nothing. I called the Audio-visual Center about a courtesy phone, and they thought I was loony! A student came down to the first floor of Crowell Hall and informed me that this was a hoax! When I returned to class, everyone was laughing heartily! Later, during this class, the same voice as before announced over the P. A. system, "Dr. Nevin, the Force is with you. Tell us a Timothy story!" I did. (A Timothy story was about something humorous or remarkable that our son Timothy said or did when he was a little boy.) After class, the voice said, "Merry Christmas, Dr. Nevin!" Someone had made a tape recording and plugged it into the public address system for that room! The student who did this sat at the very back of a long classroom and had the tape player covered.

Before 1982, we sometimes got temporary roll books on the first day of class, and sometimes we didn't. The temporary roll books would have to suffice up to five weeks. But in 1982 we experienced a phenomenal event—permanent roll books on the first day of class! That was delightful! A heroic effort by the Registrar's Office made this possible, along with computerizing the process. I expressed a great deal of appreciation to the Registrar's Office for this improvement.

About once a semester we took 15 minutes of class time to hold a "Daddy cookie" party, sometimes meeting in the Kimball Room in the lower level between Crowell Hall and Smith Hall. We gave each student a huge oatmeal and coconut cookie, a full meal in one cookie! I usually baked these myself for our own children. Because of this and because of their enormous size, we called them Daddy cookies. Sometimes the female students would take a bite, then wrap the rest in a Kleenex for future enjoyment, since one cookie proved too large for a light snack!

B. Student Homework

During my 32 years on the Moody faculty, the students changed in some ways. In the early years, studies were a high priority; in later years, too many other interests competed severely for the students' attention. The academic standards were always demanding at Moody. In my earlier years, students were willing to accept these high standards and give their best efforts. In later years, many students were a little less willing to sacrifice their own comforts to accomplish their academic responsibilities. But one factor never changed. Students (and sometimes, teachers) tended to procrastinate while deadlines approached steadily. I wrote in my 1995 diary, "I had a pack of bleary-eyed students in New Testament Synthesis [survey], worn and bedraggled. They brought in their term papers as if they were carrying the "Hope" diamond. Many are still hoping."

On another occasion, I was proctoring a final exam for one of my classes, when one of my students, a relatively new Christian, brought a bird to class, wrapped in a towel. The bird had been injured when it flew into the single men's dorm (Culbertson Hall). The student was a warm hearted young man who found the bird in the shower room, captured it, and was nursing it back to health. He brought the bird to me, and asked me to hold it for him while he took his exam. So I did so! Some of the students laughed; others smiled. But all took their exam.

C. Courses I Taught

Sometimes people might get the impression that each professor teaches the same small variety of courses during his or her whole career—courses narrowly restricted to the one or two fields of the professor's expertise. This is usually true, but I taught a wide range of courses during my 32 years at Moody. Most of the assigned courses were given me because of my interest and ability in Bible and theology. But once in a while, a course was assigned because someone was needed to teach it. (This happens in other colleges as well.) I sometimes laughingly remarked, "I've taught everything at Moody except knitting!" Actually, almost all of my courses fit into either Bible or theology in some way. A table of the courses I taught follows. The numbers in parentheses show how many semesters I taught each course listed. The courses in italics are ones I personally developed and got accepted into the Day School curriculum. The underlined numbers show the total number of <u>different</u> courses I taught over 32 years, and the total number of courses in each division.

Day School Classes (1963-1995)	Evening School Classes (1963-82)	Summer School Classes (1969-88)	Women's Guild Classes (1963-69)
Personal Evangelism (8)	Doctrine of Man and Salvation (1)	Personal Evangelism (1)	Cults (1)
New Testament Synthesis (5)	Exposure of False Systems (Cults and Isms in the Light of the Bible) (5)	Bible Study Methods (1)	Philippians, Colossians, Philemon (1)
Old Testament Synthesis (2)	Philippians, Colossians, Philemon (1)	Significant Cities in Biblical History (2)	Hebrews, James (1)
Introductory Greek Grammar (2)	How to Interpret the Bible (Principles for Interpreting the Bible) (9)	Romans (1)	1 Peter, 2 Peter, Jude (1)
Hermeneutics (33)	Personal Evangelism (How to Share Your Faith) (3)		Book of Revelation (1)
Prison Epistles (1)	Galatians, James (2)		Doctrine of the Bible and God (1)
Prison and Pastoral Epistles (2)	How to Study the Bible on Your Own (8)		Bible Survey: Isaiah to Daniel (1)
Genesis (7)	Evidences that the Bible is the Word of God (1)		Bible Survey: Minor Prophets (1)
Systematic Theology: Bibliology, Theology Proper, Anthropology (56)	New Testament Survey: Matthew to Galatians (1)		The Doctrine of God (1)
Systematic Theology: Christology, Soteriology (38)	General Epistles (1)		The Doctrine of Angels (1)
Bible Study Methods (18)	Personal Evangelism (How to Share Your Faith) (3)		The Doctrine of the Holy Spirit (1)
Gospel of John (1)	Doctrine of Salvation (1)		New Testament Survey (Eph. to Rev.) (1)
Modern Religious Movements (1967) (8)	Discovering Your Spiritual Gifts (8)		Bible Survey: Hebrews to Rev. (1)
Theology Seminar (2)			Bible Survey: Matt to Romans (1)
Hermeneutics/Bible Study Methods (1977) (43)			
Elements of Bible Study (1983) (14)			
16 different courses; 240 total courses	**13 different courses; 44 total courses**	**4 different courses; 5 total courses**	**14 different courses; 14 total courses**

Grand Totals: <u>47 different</u> courses; <u>303 total</u> courses; approximately 10,000 students

CHAPTER 6
TEACHER AS FRIEND

A. Current Students as Friends

Carol and I were very sensitive to the fact that our students lived in cramped dormitories, attended many classes, studied a lot, and were so busy that they seldom had a chance to get away from campus, which in the early days consisted of two blocks of brick, steel, and cement. I had too many students to really disciple every one of them. This was unfortunate, since part of Moody's educational philosophy was for teachers to disciple students so they would become disciplined followers of Christ. And so, we made it a point to invite students out to our home in West Chicago for a meal and a relaxing time of ping pong, table games, and visiting. We made many student friends in this way, and they were extremely grateful for an opportunity to get better acquainted with at least one of their teachers and a faculty wife! Later, as our children grew, the students enjoyed relating to our kids as well. We continued this practice for many years, and the hours we spent in a relaxed atmosphere with our students became some of our fondest memories. We did this anywhere from once a week to once a month or less, depending upon where we could fit it in, and when the students were available. We usually had students out on a Friday evening or Saturday afternoon. They were happy to discover that we were also human, and these experiences often helped to shape their attitudes toward classes, teachers, and the Moody Bible Institute. They remembered these occasions with gratitude for many years to come.

On a Friday in late October 1973, I led twelve students down the mile and a quarter to the Chicago and Northwestern Train Station, where we boarded the train for Winfield. We were all hiking the one and three fourths miles from the Winfield Station to our house in unincorporated West Chicago. The only problem was that I led them down the wrong trail to a short distance from our house, and we ended up on the wrong side of the DuPage River! So we had to return to Winfield to get the correct trail! There is a lake about three blocks east of our home, called Spring Lake, and one of the students mistook the mossy water for grass, stepped on "the grass" and got quite wet! When we finally arrived, we had marshmallows around a campfire with guitars and singing. We had all twelve students sleep outdoors, the guys in the tent and the gals in sleeping bags near the tree house. But three gals gave up on the outdoor life and crept inside the house during the 40-degree night temperature. Saturday was planned to be a workday, where the students volunteered to help faculty members in whatever ways they needed assistance. On Saturday morning at 7:00 a.m. I sounded the gong and prepared pancakes for breakfast. By 8 everyone was busy. One group weeded flowerbeds and terrace steps, another group painted storm windows, and a third group prepared the basement for painting. One student had brought a van out to our house, so we loaded everyone in it, plus Tim and Ruth, and went to Wheaton College to watch the last soccer game of the season, played between Moody and Wheaton *in the rain*! Coming back to our house, we all had a nice buffet dinner, including grilled hamburgers. Then we painted the interior basement walls. The Moody students helped us greatly and we all had a wonderful time!

One Saturday in 1978, we had about 26 students, 2 wives of students, 5 children, and 2 faculty members and their wives out for the afternoon and evening. Our guests totaled around 37. The faculty couples helped us entertain the students. We played kicker (similar to foosball), Frisbee, and two-hand touch football. We served grilled hamburgers, hot dogs, sloppy joes, jello salads, and a tossed salad. We also had a marshmallow roast and hot chocolate around a bonfire. We took some of the students for a walk in the nearby forest preserve. In the evening, Carol and I showed our transparencies and told the story of the carpenter and the tinker, taken from the children's book, *The Checker Players*, by Alan Venable. We also told the story of our romance.

We cooperated with the Dean's Department in having students overnight with us or spend the weekend with us when they were depressed or close to burnout. We developed some strong friendships in this way, and the students were glad to have the opportunity to leave the big city for the suburbs. Here they saw trees, grass, and flowers, and got to know Carol and me (and later, our children), in our home. It was a chance to relax and to see their teacher in a setting outside the classroom. I am certain that some of our greatest influence on students came from these occasions. One student spent an afternoon and overnight with us, and I got her up at 5:00 a.m. to catch the train back to Moody so we both could make our first classes. She vowed she'd never complain about 8:00 a.m. classes again! We often had students out to our house for holidays also, such as Thanksgiving or Christmas or Easter, especially foreign students and others who were unable to be with their families.

We hired one of my students, George Law, to help us tile the living room ceiling and replace the living room drywall. He and his brother worked on this project for several weeks in their "spare time." I worked with them whenever I could spare a few hours. We later hired a graduate, Jim Hamilton, a carpenter from Springfield, Illinois, to do some interior repairs and build a fence around the back yard for our dog. We kept this pen for many years, until the last of our dogs had died.

One student even stayed in the guest room at our home for three weeks while waiting for a dormitory room at Moody to be available. Of course, I related to many students who came to see me in my office as well. Some came for counseling about personal matters. Others came for help on assignments, to check on a grade, or for assistance on next semester's classroom schedule. (Each faculty member was assigned ten to twenty students whose major was in their department, to help them plan their classroom schedules and give preliminary approval to schedules before the students went to the Registrar's Office to register.) Some came with prayer requests. Some were grieving because they had lost a loved one. Others came for a bit of reassurance that they really should be at Moody. A few came to say goodbye if they were taking a permanent departure.

Some came to say thank you for a meaningful lesson or some special attention I had given to their needs. They came for all sorts of reasons, and I tried to give them my full attention and to encourage them as much as possible. Sometimes they made appointments, and, at other times, just dropped in unannounced. I took time if at all possible. When it was not possible to see them immediately, I tried to re-schedule them for a slot in the near future.

Sometimes we were able to help married students or other friends when they had to move from one apartment or house to another. Of course, we attended many weddings of my former students or Carol's student friends.

I always took a special interest in my minority students, such as African Americans, Africans, Hispanics and Native Americans. I felt we had too few of these people in our student body, but I was glad to see that the numbers gradually increased. I encouraged our administrators and especially the Admissions Office to be on the lookout for potential students among racial minorities, to help these students academically, and to encourage them to persevere. Sometimes the results were heartening, but more often, disappointing. Often our minority students did not have a very good scholastic background and found it hard to cope with Moody's academic standards and culture. I felt that, as a school, we did not do enough to assist them.

For several years I helped advise the Pulpit Club by attending its meetings and assisting with the planning. The Pulpit Club was a student organization designed to hear pastors from successful churches, and absorb ideas and inspiration for preaching, evangelistic outreach, church planting, and other pastoral work. The Pulpit Club met once a month.

I had the privilege of attending the Urbana Missions Conference in December 1973, and I was invited to be present at an MBI Alumni meeting at a local church in Champaign/Urbana. Of the 45 present, two-thirds of them were either my former students or current students. What a thrill!

About once a week I joined the students in the dining hall and had a meal with them. In later years, our administration saw the need for more of this activity, and provided meal tickets to encourage this kind of interaction. I had some profitable discussions with students at our table. I usually sat at a different table each week.

We also ran across MBI graduates here and there, not only in the Chicago metropolitan area, but elsewhere as well. In 1977, our family had a wonderful vacation in California. We ate lunch at a McDonald's in Fullerton, CA, where Mission Aviation Fellowship had its headquarters at the time. Carol spotted three families that "looked like missionaries," she said. She also thought they looked like Moody graduates. "What does a Moody graduate look like?" I puzzled. I saw two of them praying over their food, so I introduced myself. I soon discovered that one person in each family had been a student of mine at Moody! One family was back from Zaire, and the other two from Brazil. Each of the men was a missionary pilot with MAF. Once, when we attended the Church of the Open Door in Los Angeles, we saw a couple of Moody students in the pew in front of us. They had been in my classes as well!

In 1981, the students from one of my classes generously gave me a copy of the *New American Standard Exhaustive Concordance of the Bible*. I had each student sign it, and it has been a cherished possession.

On a few occasions, I sensed that the homework I assigned was excessive, and the students were beginning to get discouraged with their heavy load. And so, when I felt that I had been a bit unfair, and student morale needed improvement, I reduced the semester's assignments. On one occasion in 1982, I announced what I called "Pope Paul's Papal Proclamation," in which I eliminated two of the eight papers I had assigned. I received a hearty applause!

Grateful students observed Teacher Appreciation Day once each spring. We faculty members received candy and appreciation cards in our boxes, sometimes a carnation, balloons and student–made signs on our office doors, etc. There were special songs and skits in class in some years. Many students gave personal words of thanks to their professors. It was a nice custom that reminded us that our friendships with students were reciprocal.

In March 1988, student Dan Matthewson came by my office and presented me with the "Red Jello Award" for "having a positive impact on a world that is not so positive." The Social Deviate, an underground newspaper that was circulated by a dozen students, sponsored this award. One of our son's poems was in it, along with my photo. I was proud of this award!

B. Graduates and Former Students as Friends

Even after my students had graduated or left the Institute, they often came to see me in later years. Some had become missionaries, or pastors, or youth leaders. Some were active lay people in their churches. Others worked for Christian organizations. They appreciated our family's influence on their lives while they were students and wanted to renew those relationships. Sometimes they were discouraged in their Christian living or in their Christian service and needed encouragement. Other times they just wanted to thank us for our input into their lives, or to share some of their life's victories. We enjoyed these visits and admonished them to persevere in good works, knowing that they would reap a great harvest if they did not grow weary in well doing (taken from Gal. 6:9).

C. Students as Critics

Not every Moody student thought I was an adequate teacher. Each semester, out of 150-200 students, I would have one or two critics that gave me a hard time in class. I tried to listen to their objections and profit from them. Some of their objections were very reasonable. Some, from my biased perspective, were not. In November 1992, one of my students came by the office and asked if he was being offensive in class. I said "yes," and invited him in. He wondered what I thought of him, and I replied that I thought he was very immature, even childish, and socially insensitive. He became angry, hurt, and resentful. He then said that I came across to him as an old fuddy-duddy, a know-it-all who wants his students to shut up and listen! I pondered that for quite awhile! Later, I asked this student to forgive me for my critical attitude toward him. He asked me to pray that he would be able to forgive me.

Another student came to my office and said he already knew everything I taught in a particular course, that he considered my material elementary, so he decided to quit my class. That was very unusual indeed! Quite a number of students (about 5% in my Hermeneutics/Bible Study Methods courses) dropped this class because they felt the material was too demanding, the homework too time-consuming. As I look back, I tend to agree with these latter critics, and wish I could have simplified the assignments so the students could enjoy them more and would have adopted more of the methods as their permanent Bible study procedures.

D. The Moody Family as Friends

One of the nicest things about Moody Bible Institute was the lasting friendships we enjoyed with fellow faculty members, students, employees, and sometimes, administrators.

In my early years of teaching, the Moody faculty had a tradition of playing volleyball over the noon hour in the tiny "cracker box" gym located in Norton Hall. Dr. Culbertson, our president, was one of the most enthusiastic players, and he had a wicked serve! David Smart of the music department was also an excellent player, as was Gene Getz. I can still hear Gene Getz calling out, "Change of pace!" when his team was losing. In November 1964, a medical incident occurred while we were playing volleyball with just two on a team. Harry Dixon Loes of the Music Department suffered a stroke. He recovered for a time, but passed away a few months later.

This faculty volleyball tradition continued for many years, until the growth of the student body required two lunch hours instead of one. In 1966, Jack Wyrtzen's male quartet, all of them Moody grads, challenged the faculty to a volleyball game. The quartet had been undefeated for 205 games straight! The students packed our little gym to cheer the teams, and there was much excitement. The quartet won the first game, but the faculty won the second and third games. What a thrill!

Faculty members and other employees who were woodworking enthusiasts were invited to Mr. H. C. Crowell's home (son of H. P. Crowell of Quaker Oats fame, for whom Crowell Hall was named) in Winnetka, Illinois on Saturday evenings. (To learn more about H.

P. Crowell, see *Cereal Tycoon*, by Joe Musser, published in 1997 by Moody Press.)

Omar Brubaker, a tall, broad shouldered man with a big heart for God, had his office near mine in Fitzwater Hall. He taught Christian education and Bible subjects. He invited me to meet with him for a weekly half-hour devotional study of Scripture and a brief prayer time. We did this for several years until each of us became too rushed to schedule it. It was a mutual blessing. Omar was my best man at our wedding. He had a lovely wife who liked to paint illustrations for children's stories. Omar's initials were J.O.B. They had four beautiful daughters, whom I called "Job's Daughters." On his retirement dinner in 1994, three of his four daughters were present with their husbands. Daughter Beverly read his biographical sketch and cried when she came to his illness. Omar had to be released from the hospital in order to attend this important ceremony. Omar was a good friend over the years, until his untimely death from leukemia (bone marrow cancer) in 1996. He had experienced a miraculous recovery from this disease that the doctors could not explain. But eventually, after successfully fighting it for many years, he had a relapse that was fatal.

The four faculty members who were hired in 1963, plus John Tahl, of Practical Christian Ministries, used to meet every five years for a dinner and celebration of the Lord's blessings upon our ministries. One of the nicest occasions was when we celebrated our 25th anniversary at Moody by eating at the Country Squire in Grayslake, Illinois in May 1988. This restaurant with its lovely setting was a place where former governors of Illinois had eaten. The Brubakers, the Nevins, Rosemary Turner, and John Tahl were present. Sadly, Robert Goddard had already passed away. Our last special meal for our 30th anniversary of service at Moody was held in Lemont at the White Fence Farm, a rustic restaurant with old museum pieces and old clocks on the wall. Only the Brubakers and the Nevins were present.

I am reminded that of the four faculty members who were hired at the same time, three of us developed cancer. Omar Brubaker and Dr. Robert Goddard died from it, and Rosemary Turner recovered from it.

Another good friend was Al Classen, a Mennonite with a heart for God and missions. As a young man, he served as a missionary in Nigeria and taught in a seminary there. He and his wife, Evelyn, had three fine sons. Our two families took a joint vacation in the Wisconsin woods in July 1967, when our son Timothy was only a few weeks old. I also met Dr. Louis Goldberg, who taught Old Testament, Hebrew, and Jewish Studies. We became lifelong friends. I came to know and appreciate every faculty member, but some were closer than others. I was saddened when Dr. Douglas Stephens, my faculty neighbor across from my office in Fitzwater Hall for many years, passed away on November 9, 1994.

For some years, the faculty had faculty prayer meetings where we shared our concerns and prayed for one another, for our administrators, students, and employees.

When a faculty member retired, a farewell dinner was held for him or her. These farewell dinners were very special occasions, with a fine meal, speeches of appreciation from administrators and faculty friends, and gifts and a plaque for the retiree. They were held in one of the private dining rooms on campus, and were limited to some thirty-five guests, most of whom were chosen by the faculty member retiring.

The whole Moody family was shocked when Ralph Patterson of the Music Department passed away suddenly at his home. I had played volleyball with him many times. Another trauma for us all was the unexpected death of Dr. Coleman Luck, chair of the Bible Department. He slipped and fell on the ice in the winter of 1976, breaking his leg. He developed a blood clot in his lung after surgery to remove the cast on his leg. He passed away in March of that year.

We made friends with employees, too. John and Barbara Tahl became good friends. Barbara was a nurse and John assisted the director of the Practical Christian Ministries Department. Since we belonged to the same church, (Calvary Memorial Church of Oak Park), and they lived nearby, the Tahls invited us to dinner many a Wednesday evening before going to the church prayer meeting.

Talent Night at Moody was an annual event that brought faculty, staff and employees together to see one another's (sometimes) hidden talents and hobbies. It was a lot of fun and led to good socializing throughout the Institute.

When we invited students to come to visit us at our house, we usually had from three to six students out at one time, although there were exceptions when we invited an entire class out and served a picnic style meal. Sometimes, in good weather, we would have a bonfire downhill in our West Chicago back yard and a marshmallow roast. We would sing gospel songs and choruses together to the accompaniment of a guitar. When we met inside the house, we would have table games, table tennis, foosball, and round robin. Round robin is a table tennis game where any number can play. The participants are divided evenly at each end of the table. The person who is "up" hits the ball gently over the net, lays the racquet on the table, and immediately runs to the other end of the table and gets in line behind other players. Each player is allowed five misses ("boo-boos"), after which he or she is eliminated. The game gets wilder and wilder when there are only four or three players left. When all but two players are eliminated, they stay at their end of the table, but must spin a complete circle and try to hit the ball after they have spun. Those who get dizzy easily get wiped out quickly! The round robin games were always hilarious and the laughter was refreshing!

Moody has a solid reputation for training missionaries. We had many missionary friends, and they would sometimes stop in to see us when they were in the Chicago area. Some we hosted for a day or two; others, several days, and still others, just a few hours. Some of these missionaries we knew from previous contacts in former churches, both in Illinois and in California. Other missionary friends were graduates of Moody Bible Institute, many of them former students of mine.

During the early years, Carol often attended the faculty wives' meetings. She used this opportunity to get acquainted with other wives of faculty members.

Leisure was scarce at Moody. We had a work ethic, and everyone—students, teachers, employees, and administrators were all expected to work hard and to be productive. But some leisure is essential to well being.

The old Sweet Shop, long since replaced by the Coffee Cove, was a favorite spot for faculty, employees, and even students to meet for mid-morning snacks. Today's Coffee Cove, located in the Alumni Center, is the third such place in my experience. Many a friendship was nourished by the fellowship and food at the Cove. Once, a funny thing happened while several of us faculty members were having snacks. One professor bought a piece of toast; another secretly snatched it and gave it to me. I inadvertently ate it, thinking it a gift from the second prof!

Another time, in 1976, I played a trick on our president, Dr. Sweeting, in the Coffee Cove. I had a wound-up rubber band tied to two ends of a paper clip with a piece of cardboard stapled to the paper clip's middle. These were enclosed in an unsealed envelope. I put the envelope into Dr. Sweeting's hand, asking him, "Would you like to see some rattlesnake eggs?" When he opened the envelope, the contents sprang out and rattled like a rattlesnake! Dr. Sweeting was startled, but soon enjoyed a laugh. I wrote in my diary that day, "It was nice working at Moody!"

Once a year, the MBI administration sponsored a family outing for all full-time employees and their families. Family Day was held on a Saturday, usually in October. One location used was Santa's Village in Elgin; another was Enchanted Forest, at Porter, Indiana, fifteen miles east of Gary. Sometimes the weather was chilly, but we always had a good time with other faculty members, non-faculty employees, and their families. Single employees were permitted to invite a guest. These outings were great occasions to get to know other employees better.

Another very nice custom was the annual employee's Christmas party held in the dining hall. All employees, including faculty members, were treated to tasty refreshments and Christmas music during coffee break time. An administrator would express appreciation for the entire Moody family. We greatly enjoyed this gesture of good will from the administration.

All faculty and employees who have worked for Moody for 25 years or more are automatically members of the Diamond Pin Club. (Recently, this privilege has been extended to those who have worked less than 25 years.) After I became a member, I attended my first annual Diamond Pin Club banquet in 1989. At that time, we bought our own meals and carried them to the meeting place. Later, MBI sponsored an annual catered banquet for the Diamond Pin Club. When the Institute became pressed for money, this became an every other year event, which it still is today. A program of singing and entertainment always followed the meal. Members were given a copy of the letters written by those unable to attend and others who wanted to share their past year's happenings with us.

CHAPTER 7
THE TEACHER AS
ACADEMIC

A. Academic Enrichment

Much of my academic growth came from my reading of books in the biblical and theological subject areas. This was greatly accelerated during my four years of being editor for *Moody Monthly*'s book review column. I also grew academically while researching for a thorough text on the integration of hermeneutics and Bible study methods. In 1969, Paul Snezek, then MBI's head librarian, and I launched the Faculty Book Forum. It was a discussion group composed of faculty colleagues that met once a month and considered an important biblical or theological topic dealt with by an important newer book. Each faculty member who attended was supposed to read the book and be ready to discuss the issues raised by it. We had some very good discussions on these key books for a year or two, until most Faculty Book Forum members got too busy to prepare. We finally disbanded the club.

I became a member of the Evangelical Theological Society in 1964 and attended many of its national and regional meetings. The national conferences were at first held at various Christian colleges and seminaries in different parts of the United States. Later, they were held in hotels. The Midwest regional conferences were smaller and shorter in length, but still profitable. Often a paper on a theological or biblical theme would spark my interest to study the topic further. These conferences offered many opportunities to update our awareness and information on theological issues, make new academic friends, interact with scholars from other schools, and to purchase theological books at a considerable discount! Moody was usually able to provide funding to attend these conferences, and this was much appreciated. Faculty members who were sent to various conferences, seminars, or short-term missions would give a brief report in a faculty meeting upon their return.

I had some interest in philosophy, so I decided in 1986 to attend a philosophy conference at Wheaton College. I enjoyed hearing some important Christian philosophers, but was not impressed with their communication skills. The technical jargon plus the flat delivery of most papers helped me to decide that philosophy conferences weren't very exciting. I never attended one since.

One of the most meaningful conferences I attended was in 1987, a four-day conference sponsored jointly by the Institute for Advanced Christian Studies of American Evangelicals (IFACS) and the Institute for the Study of American Evangelicals (ISAE), held at the Barrows Auditorium, Wheaton College. The following were the main speakers:

- George Marsden, a keen student of evangelicalism (Duke University)
- David Livingstone (Queens University, Belfast), on natural science
- Elving Anderson (University of Minnesota), also on natural science
- James Skillen (Association for Public Justice), on political science
- David Richardson (University of Wisconsin, Madison), on economics
- Carl F. H. Henry, "a theologian's theologian" and founding editor of *Christianity Today*, on Christian scholarship
- Robert Wuthnow (Princeton University), on sociology
- Mary Stewart Van Leeuwen (Calvin College), on psychology
- Patricia Ward (Wheaton College), on literature
- Nicholas Wolterstorff a Christian philosopher (Calvin College), on creative arts.

I also was thrilled to meet Bernard Ramm, many of whose books I had read; and Carl F. H. Henry. The conference forced me to think about issues in an interdisciplinary way. The speakers represented a good balance of viewpoints between professors from secular universities and those from Christian colleges and graduate schools.

B. Continuing Education

Although I already had a doctorate in theology, I often wished I could top off my education with a Ph.D. degree. I began a master's program in philosophy at Roosevelt University, but decided after three courses that it was not what I wanted. I also took two summer courses in education at Northern Illinois University, but decided not to pursue a doctorate in education. The education courses did not actually make me a better teacher, and some of them seemed to magnify details into courses with little substance. I decided I could learn methodology and process improvements on my own while teaching.

I profited greatly from an intensive two-week course (four and a half hours daily for ten days) from Dr. Merrill Tenney of Wheaton College on inductive Bible study. This became my foundation for teaching Bible Study Methods at Moody, supplemented by much reading in various texts on inductive Bible study.

MBI's administration has been very supportive of faculty members who sought advanced degrees. This was especially true of those who had master's degrees but lacked a doctorate. In my own case, I already had a doctor's degree, but sought a second master's degree to broaden myself in psychology and philosophy and to review some theological disciplines. Our administration graciously consented to provide half of my tuition for this endeavor. I began my M.A. program in Interdisciplinary Studies at Wheaton Graduate School in 1983 and continued, one course at a time, through 1989. I was even permitted to skip faculty meetings one year in order to get the course I needed. At the same time that I was working on my M.A. degree, I was teaching full-time at Moody. It proved to be very strenuous, but also very profitable. My life during that time was more hectic than usual! I took courses in philosophy, psychology, and biblical studies. This was possible only because most of my Moody classes were in the morning, and I was able to get afternoon classes at Wheaton Graduate School that would meet the requirements. I would take the train to Moody, teach classes, hurry back to the train and commute to Wheaton, take classes there, then catch a train again for home. Soon after graduating in 1989, I had my first heart attack and first stroke

CHAPTER 8
MY WORK IN THE OFFICE

A. Correcting Papers

When I was a boy, I dreamed of becoming a teacher so I could correct student papers and exams. Little did I realize that paper correcting was the bane of every teacher! Writing papers is often the best way the student can learn course material, and both papers and exams will help measure the student's progress. However, correcting these papers is very time-consuming and soon becomes boring, since there is a drab similarity in their content! The few exceptions, where students show creativity and resourcefulness, are refreshing. Many teachers use so-called objective exams, such as multiple-choice, true or false, matching, and the like, but even these have to be tallied and entered into the grade book. Raw scores must be transformed into letter grades, and a host of data entered into the grade book. I always prepared my own exams, together with a key for correcting them. I discovered that objective exams are not as objective as they seem; there is always room for debate on some questions in every exam. I also discovered that essay exams were a better way to find out what a student really understands. But where the class size exceeded 30 or 40, essay exams became self-punishment for the teacher!

In the 60's and 70's, papers were written in ink; there were no personal computers available until about 1980. During my second year of teaching, I had piled these papers on my kitchen table for correcting. The window next to the table was open about an inch.

During the night, snow blew in through that inch of open window and covered all my students' hermeneutics papers. About 80 of them were wet, and a dozen of them ruined, as the melted snow made the ink illegible! I spread them out on paper towels over the kitchen floor to dry. I was ashamed to announce in class that I had ruined some of their papers, but they thought it was very funny! I wrote in 1978: "It seems as though of the correcting of papers there is no end!" I often had to catch up on correcting papers during Christmas and Easter breaks. This left little time for relaxing with the family or short vacations.

B. Grading

Ask any teacher what is the least favorite part of his or her vocation, and most of them will tell you it is correcting papers! Perhaps the second least favorite thing is semester-end grading. After all classes are finished for the semester, and the students are enjoying their vacation time, the teachers must slave away at finalizing the grade of each student and turn into the Registar's Office the completed grade books, working against a deadline of about one week or, at the most, two. Sometimes a grade must be delayed because the student has not yet turned in all requirements. At other times, a student is dissatisfied about his or her grade, and complains to the teacher. This further delays the completing of the grade books. If any grades are turned in late, the teacher hears from the registrar or even the academic dean. The pressure is on! The Registrar's Office cannot record the grades in the permanent records until all teachers have turned in all their grades. Meanwhile, the students wonder when they will get their final grade report! In 1973, after completing my semester grading, I wrote, "Some [students] came by and wept; others rejoiced."

Since my first year of teaching in 1963, I have sensed a very gradually increasing grade inflation problem among the faculty. At the same time, I felt that grade inflation was becoming an increasingly serious problem throughout our nation's educational system. Moody does have high standards, and our grade inflation has, in my opinion, been less severe than in many other colleges, universities, and graduate schools. Unfortunately, the easiest course of action was to ignore the grade inflation problem, so very little was done to correct it during my 32-year Moody career. For several years, the academic dean published among the faculty the total number of A's, B's, C's, D's and F's given by each faculty member to his or her students. This allowed us to compare our grading performance with that of other faculty members. But faculty members whose grading was too soft or too hard strongly resisted any suggestion that they should change their grading methods, and it became such a sensitive matter that administrators applied very little pressure.

I was known as a tough grader, and I am unrepentant! I believed strongly that students must *earn* good grades; they are not to be *given* them. I was very happy to give A's to those who really deserved them, and I did not hesitate to give D's or F's to those whose work was poor. Students frequently asked me if I graded "on a curve." The classic bell curve allowed 10% A's, 20% B's, 40% C's, 20% D's, and 10% F's. I never did use this method of grading. Instead, I developed five or six different percentage scales, using the scale that matched best a given class' performance. Sometimes I granted a second chance to students who did poorly on an exam or on their papers. This might take the form of extra reading, an extra paper, or an extra exam.

Most of the time I favored multiple-choice exams. In fact, I spent much of every summer revising course requirements, exams, quizzes, and grading keys. I also chose and ordered textbooks and collateral reading. I revised syllabi, handouts, and bibliographies, and tried to improve content and teaching methods so that the next time, my courses would show improvements.

Beginning in 1986, for several years I used essay exams. I believe these are superior instruments to find out what a student has learned. The only problem is, essays take a very long time to correct and I already had too much to do! So, I was forced to go back to multiple-choice exams to avoid seriously overloading myself.

C. Developing Courses

In 1967, I developed and taught a course called Modern Religious Movements. It included Roman Catholicism, Judaism, and the larger Protestant cults or sects I viewed as unorthodox. The students found this course useful in their witness to others and in their Practical Christian Ministries assignments. It is still taught in the World Missions major.

My friend, Phil Lueck, taught at Grace Bible Institute (now called Grace University), in Omaha; Greenville College, in Greenville, Illinois; and Northwestern College, in Minneapolis/St. Paul. The year was 1974, and Phil persuaded me to work with him in integrating biblical hermeneutics with Bible study methods. Biblical hermeneutics teaches the theory and practice of accurately interpreting the Bible. Up to this time, these courses were usually taught as separate disciplines. We called the new course "Metheneutics" to suggest that Bible study methods and hermeneutics were being combined. Phil Lueck pioneered this course in the schools where he taught, while I pioneered it at Moody, beginning in 1977. The Moody catalog listed the course as Hermeneutics/ Bible Study Methods. The course proved to be very popular, and because we limited it to 30 students, it required two or three sections to meet the demand. Phil found it to be much appreciated also in the three schools where he taught it. Our first trial version included 300 pages of mimeographed notes that the students used as a textbook.

This course is still required of all majors except Missionary Aviation and Sacred Music majors.

In the year1983, I developed and began teaching a course called Elements of Bible Study. It was designed for freshmen, who requested that they be introduced to hermeneutics and Bible study methods in their first year in college. It had some material that was also found in Hermeneutics/Bible Study Methods, limited to juniors and seniors. But Elements of Bible Study was a much simpler course, and omitted many things contained in the advanced course, "Metheneutics." Soon, Elements of Bible Study was required of almost all freshmen, and this necessitated seven or eight sections, taught by various professors. After many years of teaching this course, my academic dean wanted me to re-package the freshman course and discontinue the advanced course. I resisted this idea, feeling that we could not teach the more advanced methods and principles to first year students. Today, the Elements of Bible Study course is taught to Missionary Aviation majors.

D. Acting as Resource Person

The evangelical Christian public has placed a great deal of trust in the Moody Bible Institute over the years. As a result, many people phone in questions or write letters of inquiry as they seek answers to their biblical, theological and personal problems. School administrators cannot answer all of these questions, so they request the assistance of faculty members. I would occasionally be asked to take a personal call from a person who needed a biblical or theological answer for his or her problem. In addition, I always had two or three letters on my desk that I was asked to respond to. Never content with a superficial answer, I would spend hours in research when necessary to answer these letters adequately. I considered it a ministry to the friends of the Moody Bible Institute and an expression of our gratitude to donors who made Moody's work possible.

At other times, we faculty members were asked to do research for the administration in committees. Sometimes, I readily appreciated the value of this work, but at other times it seemed of little value. My estimate of its value depended largely upon whether administrators acted upon our conclusions after we had done our homework.

Some of the most meaningful research faculty members did was the times when we were involved in self-studies for accreditation. I led one of the committees for self-study in 1970 when our accreditation for the American Association of Bible Colleges was renewed. I participated in other self-study committees in 1986, and in 1987 or 1988.

It was not very long after I came to Moody that I got involved in reviewing books, usually for *Moody Monthly* (later known as *Moody Magazine*). This was a stimulus to keep reading, and also a great pleasure to be able to keep the books I reviewed. Pointing out a book's strengths and weaknesses was something I enjoyed, since the Lord has blessed me with good analytical ability. From 1969 to 1973, I was the book review editor for *Moody Monthly*. I was responsible to recruit or retain other reviewers and assign the books they would review. I also reviewed many books myself. The shorter reviews were called "book briefs." In addition to reviewing,

I had to approve all block ads for biblical and theological accuracy before they could be run in *Moody Monthly*. I also wrote a side bar column to introduce each month's reviews and discuss current issues. I received a small honorarium of $50.00 each month for book review work (later it was increased to $100.00), but more importantly, I acquired many books to add to my growing library. Assigning reviews of books to other professors, both inside and outside the Institute, and to other competent reviewers, helped cement many friendships. At first, the guest reviews were not reimbursed, but later, I was able to secure honoraria for those who wrote reviews and even for those who wrote book briefs (100 words or less).

Unfortunately, there was one big problem: the book reviewing editorship took twenty to thirty hours a week, and, when added to my other duties, made my work week unbearably long. During those years, I often went to my office six days a week. I became so busy and exhausted that I was short-changing my dear wife and children of the time and energy they deserved from me. After much discussion with Carol, prayer, and reflection, I decided to relinquish this extra responsibility before I suffered physical and mental burnout. (I had come very close to it by 1973.) I still continued to review a few books for the new book review editor, but without the clerical and administrative duties I had before.

For the first twenty years or so of our marriage, Carol and I were asked by the Dean of Student's Office to plan and conduct seminars for engaged couples and for married students. We enjoyed doing this together, and the students really appreciated our efforts. We tried to be honest about both the romantic aspects of engagement and marriage, and about the tensions we faced as a married couple, and our ways of dealing with issues. We encouraged married students to practice communication skills and spend quality time together. In 1988, Carol and I were invited to present a seminar to the Married Students' Fellowship in North Hall. We first joined in their potluck dinner, and then talked about spouse acceptance and problem solving. I showed my hat collection to illustrate eccentricity and the importance of accepting each other's uniqueness. Afterward, we talked with various married students for an hour.

E. Counseling

I soon learned that the students expected me to be able to counsel them about personal issues, even though I had no special training in psychology or counseling. The first student who came for counseling was a young woman who had no assurance of her salvation until she came to MBI. I carefully explained how to know Jesus Christ personally and how to be certain of one's salvation. She responded very warmly. Moody did have a staff of trained counselors and they regularly helped many students. But sometimes the students preferred to seek out their teachers for biblical insights and personal encouragement. We tried to help them as much as we could, but also referred them to professional counselors in situations where we were inexperienced or where more in-depth sessions were needed. Although this is unusual, occasionally students have matriculated at Moody who were confused about the way of salvation. In the fall of 1964, I prayed with a young lady who was engaged to be married. She said she had no burden for those who are lost, and wondered why. Apparently she had never received Jesus Christ as Savior and Lord. I prayed with her in my office, and then she prayed a simple childlike prayer, trusting the Lord Jesus for her salvation. What a thrill! Now she would have something to share with others. Of course, I was always available to talk with students about academic matters, homework assignments, and grades. One day I headed my diary, "Students In, Students Out; Students All About." In the early years, faculty members were required to be in their offices and available to students about 25 hours a week! This later changed, and the faculty members were free to set their own office hours, provided the hours were posted on the office door.

CHAPTER 9
OTHER TEACHING RESPONSIBILITIES

Most of us faculty members were rushed just to prepare and teach classes, relate to students in and out of the classroom, prepare exams, and grade exams and papers. There were also special projects such as radio broadcasting, preaching, writing books or correspondence courses, etc. For me, it was quite a stressful experience to get syllabi and exams ready for Moody's Copy Service ahead of the time they were needed in class. At first, I supplemented this service with my own gelatin duplicators. For those of you unfamiliar with this primitive device, it looked like a cookie pan with 1/2 inch sides, filled with clear gelatin. A carbon-coated master sheet containing the typing or other image for duplicating was placed face down over the gelatin pan until the image was transferred. Then the operator could duplicate the original, one page at a time by pressing a blank sheet onto the gelatin, then gently lifting it off. In 1967, I bought my own mimeograph machine. This drum type duplicator saved many hours in preparing exams, quizzes, syllabi, and handouts, and it allowed me to prepare these items on short notice, since they didn't have to go through Copy Service. We kept this duplicator at home and I spent many late nights running off handouts, quizzes, or exams!

A. Faculty Meetings

We faculty often viewed faculty meetings as a necessary disruption to our busy schedules. When I first came to Moody, faculty meetings were weekly and lasted two hours. Every committee chairperson was asked to give a report of progress, whether they had any new information or not. The meetings seemed rather boring, and all full-time faculty members were required to attend. Sometimes we did very significant business, but at other times there seemed little reason to meet. It did, however, afford us brief opportunities to relate to our colleagues whose offices were in other buildings than our own. There were some happy exceptions to the long meetings, as some of them were less than an hour. At first, we met on Monday afternoons, but in 1972 the meeting time changed to Wednesdays.

During the sixties, governance was from the top down. There was very little democracy. Faculty members were expected to fulfill their duties, and not ask too many questions of the administration. When the president spoke, discussion was ended. The faculty's vote was only advisory; the administrators made all the final decisions.

I was pleased to see that this way of governance was gradually modified over the next two decades. Faculty members were given more opportunity to express themselves, and administrators came to respect their opinions more fully about plans, procedures, and policies. Accreditation visits by the American Association of Bible Colleges, and later by the North Central Association of Colleges and Schools also encouraged this movement toward greater faculty empowerment. This is not to say that the Moody Bible Institute was run badly before this time, but in the seventies and eighties differences of opinion came more and more to be tolerated and even respected by administrators.

B. Committee Work

Committees can be efficient and productive, or occasionally, they can accomplish little. I have served on both kinds at Moody.

Most committee chairs took their work seriously, but how much is ultimately accomplished by a committee depends partly upon whether it can persuade faculty and administration of the changes that are proposed. I served on many committees at Moody, most of them as a member appointed by the administration. As the years passed, I was asked to chair quite a number of committees as well.

One committee on which I served very early in my teaching career was called "The Committee on the Discipline of Students for Cheating." From time to time, a student would be caught cheating on an assignment by copying another student's work, or looking at another student's exam. At other times, a student would voluntarily confess to cheating on a quiz, on falsely reporting assigned reading, or some other form of academic dishonesty. The committee developed guidelines for disciplining students and sometimes, counseling them. The chair would announce the committee's decision to the student and make sure the penalty was carried out. Typical penalties were for the student to lose credit for a paper, have a grade lowered, or, in more severe cases, lose credit for a course that then had to be repeated. The committee's decision took into consideration whether the student had voluntarily confessed the cheating or simply had been caught. For most students, this decision was a sobering experience. Sometimes the student would apologize, and occasionally, break down in tears. Almost always, the penalty proved beneficial, and the student did not repeat the offense.

One committee I initiated myself was the Faculty Book Forum Planning Committee, to help plan our Faculty Book Forums. In these forums, held once a month, we would discuss the content and value of some important book we had each agreed to read ahead of time.

In 1971 I was appointed to the Chapel/Assembly Planning Committee. Unfortunately, the chairman had a different agenda than the committee members, and there was sharp disagreement between the members as well. Of all the committees on which I served, this one was my least favorite, since we accomplished so little.

In 1975, three of us faculty members formed an ad-hoc committee for curriculum revision to reorganize all course offerings into 4-hour courses. Under the plan, three courses would constitute a minimum full-time load, and four courses would be a standard load. (The standard load at the time was 16 semester hours.) Some other colleges had already adopted this curricular revision. We felt strongly that this would lighten student and teacher work loads and improve the learning process. But unfortunately, we were unable to convince a majority of our colleagues or our administrators, so the plan was never implemented.

In 1976, I served on a committee to study the feasibility of beginning fall classes two days early in order to provide a fall recess at the end of October. We suggested the name, "Reformation Recess," since Martin Luther posted his ninety-five theses on the church door at Wittenberg, Germany on October 31, 1517. Despite our enthusiasm and creativity, we were unable to convince the rest of the faculty that the break was needed.

In 1981, I became chairman of the Marriage Policy Examination Committee. The marriage policy in place at the time required students not to marry while enrolled as students. This policy was later amended to require students to marry during the summer vacation *or* after graduation.

I served on the Committee on Qualifications beginning in 1982. It dealt with the students' academic standings, and determined whether students with low grade standings could continue in school. The policy was to place the student on probation after one semester of low grades, and then monitor improvements. If after two semesters, the grades were unacceptably low, the student was asked to withdraw. Students could attend summer school or evening school and attempt to raise their academic performance, and then reapply for admission into the day program. They could also appeal to be reconsidered. Due to the serious ramifications for the students, this was one of the most active committees I had been a part of, with some meetings lasting several hours.

Beginning in 1983, for several years I served on the Moody Press Textbook Committee. We met about one evening a month for dinner and business. We analyzed the direction Moody Press was taking in the textbook publishing arena, gave our advice, and made recommendations about topics, authors, and manuscripts being considered for publication. The committee consisted of professors from Wheaton College, Trinity Evangelical Divinity School, and MBI. We were rewarded by the free meal and some free books. When Moody Press decided not to emphasize textbooks any longer, this committee was disbanded.

I was placed on the Commencement Program Committee (later called the Commencement Festival Committee), where we auditioned seniors who wished to participate in the activities of Senior Class Day. This was one of my favorite committees, since it helped us get acquainted with students' talents and it got immediate results. We could enjoy those results in the Commencement Festival, which I nearly always attended. I remarked in my 1987 diary that Carol and I attended "the excellent Commencement Festival, which included not only music, but also the students whom our committee had to decide on for personal performances. Dawn Solheim did a magnificent job on a dramatic reading called "The Branch." And two students did very well on another dramatic reading named "King Me!" Students also presented a 3-minute multi-media showing the chaos and the calm of a Moody student's life.

For several years, I was the chair for a committee to coordinate Elements of Bible Study and Hermeneutics/Bible Study Methods courses. In that capacity, I met periodically with all the faculty members who taught either of those courses. Sometimes I felt frustrated because some teachers of these courses felt free to emphasize hermeneutics to the neglect of Bible study methods. I could only plead with them to strive for balance, but I had no authority to require it.

Somewhere between 1986 and 1987, I served on a self-study committee to prepare for regional accreditation. Moody Bible Institute was granted regional accreditation by the Commission on Institutions of Higher Education, North Central Association of Colleges and Schools, in 1989. This meant a great leap forward in academic recognition and in the transfer of credits to other colleges and universities.

In 1988 I served on the Academic Calendar Committee. We came up with some very good ideas, I thought, such as a mid-semester break in the fall, a quad system for 2-hour courses, and an interim between semesters. Perhaps some day Moody will try to incorporate them.

In 1988, I was appointed to the Faculty Development Committee, whose main responsibility was to structure and administer a faculty sabbatical program. Our administration supported our work fully. We were successful in telling faculty members when they qualified, and outlining the steps necessary for a one or two semester sabbatical.

Back in 1973, I was appointed chairman of Faculty Study Group 5 charged with writing faculty bylaws. After meeting a number of times, our committee concluded that we did not have enough information to accomplish the task, and we returned our assignment to Administration. Eighteen years later (1991), I was appointed the chair of a second Committee on Faculty Bylaws! We took four years and many hours, but this time our committee was successful, and both the faculty and our administrators accepted the final product that is intended to clarify the relationship and govern the cooperation between administrators and faculty in the Undergraduate Division of the Moody Bible Institute. From 1991 to my retirement in 1995, the Bylaws Committee took a huge amount of my time. It was a great relief to complete it! I suppose this was my favorite committee, largely because we had the full cooperation of our administrators and our committee members seriously committed themselves to the task. The approval process was given a full hearing and voting for approval was done one section at a time. All full-time faculty members and all educational administrators had their voices heard, and this resulted in some amendments before the full document was approved. Another reason for satisfaction is that we felt as a committee that we had accomplished major improvements and clarifications in the governance of the Undergraduate Division. Of all the committees I served on, this one far surpassed the others in the significance and magnitude of the task, and I hope, in its lasting value.

Other Committees I Served

Name	Purpose	Year
Bible Department Planning Committee	Plan new Bible courses, propose changes in content or credit hours	
In-Service Training Committee	Helping faculty improve classroom teaching, testing, library research skills	
Steering Committee of the American Association of Bible Colleges	To assist in renewing MBI's accreditation with the AABC	1970
Faculty Study Groups Committee	To coordinate the work of self-study groups in our AABC Self-Study	1970
Study Group #5	To recommend to Administration constructive changes in Undergraduate Division	1970
Faculty Resources Committee	(I have forgotten)	1970
Implementation Committee #5	To follow up on AABC Self-Study recommendations	1972
Family Night Planning Committee	To plan Family Night activities for 1972	1972
Faculty Retreat Planning Committee	To plan Faculty Retreat for 1973	1973
Student-Faculty Assemblies Committee	To plan special student-faculty assemblies, invite speaker, and coordinate these assemblies	1973
Bible-related Course Revision Committee	To revise courses in Bible-related areas	1973, 1974
Long-Range Planning Committee	To suggest goals for MBI over a 10-year period	1978
Bible Analysis Curriculum Committee	To group Bible books into courses with larger numbers of semester hours in each course	1978
Special Committee on Student Cuts	To evaluate student cut system for annual missions conference	1983-86
Standards and Conduct Committee	To assist Dean's Department by recommending policies on student lifestyles	1984
Moody Logo Committee	To investigate the Moody Logo and suggest possible changes	1987
Learning Resources Center Committee	To suggest book acquisitions, discards, and other library improvements	1993-95
NCA Steering Committee	To prepare for the self-study aimed at renewing MBI's accreditation with NCA	1993
NCA Governance Committee	A subcommittee of the NCA self-study	1993
General Education Committee	To decide which courses and how many hours would be devoted to general education in the Undergraduate School	1994-95

So, of the thirty-three committees on which I served, only six of them failed to realize their objectives. That means that more than four out of five of them were successful in accomplishing the perceived need for change. In summary, Moody used faculty committees to research and recommend possible changes, propose policies, and coordinate many events. Committees kept the faculty deeply involved in the life of the school.

C. Department Meetings

For several years I was a member of three different departments—Evangelism, Bible, and Theology. Teaching even one course in a department would make one a member of that department. And so I attended three different monthly departmental meetings as well as weekly faculty meetings. The Evangelism Department met on Monday afternoon, which, in my early career, was just before the faculty meeting. Eventually, I relinquished the Personal Evangelism course, and then I had to attend only two departmental meetings. Most faculty members belonged to only one department, or, at the most, two. Department meetings were used to evaluate the curriculum in that department, propose the introduction of new courses, and deal with various departmental issues and problems.

For most of my teaching career, however, I was a member of just two departments—The Bible Department and the Theology Department. For the last few years of my teaching at Moody, the department members were privileged to help select new colleagues for their departments. Department members met and heard from the candidate and later voted on whether he or she should be hired.

CHAPTER 10
THE TEACHER
AND FIELD WORK

A. Preaching

Along with other faculty members, I had many opportunities to preach in churches in the Chicagoland area. We were usually given a small honorarium averaging about $25.00 for our services. In addition, this practice strengthened the public relations outreach of Moody Bible Institute. In my early years at Moody, I probably preached about twice a month throughout the school year. Later, I took fewer speaking engagements as I had less available time and energy. Some of these assignments were for small, declining congregations in the inner city. A few were at larger thriving congregations in the suburbs. Most of the churches that needed help in filling the pulpit for a series of messages were without a pastor at the time. Others wanted a guest speaker while their pastor was out of town. Some of these preaching opportunities were satisfying and exhilarating, as the hearers were most appreciative. Others were disappointing or even depressing. It all depended upon how the congregation received the guest speaker, how they responded, and whether they were interested in growing in their Christian experience. Frequently I was invited to lunch after preaching in a morning service, and I enjoyed getting acquainted with one of the families in the church. On a Sunday in August 1969, I spoke in the Itasca Evangelical Free Church. To my amazement, I heard WMBI over the public address system while preaching! It was quite disruptive to me, but the congregation seemed used to it. By some quirk, the WMBI transmitter, located in Addison, Illinois, was bringing Moody Radio into the P.A. system in Itasca, some three or four miles away!

I have often heard the saying that a Christian leader should "always be ready to preach, pray, or die." I was frequently asked to pray for a public gathering in church or elsewhere without prior notice. And on rare occasions I have been asked to preach without warning. In 1975 our family was visiting relatives in Modesto (central Illinois), and the intended speaker did not show up for the Sunday morning service. Two of the church leaders suddenly asked me to speak! A young lady was to sing a solo just before the message, and she was already singing it. I hoped she would sing at least six verses while I tried to reproduce an outline from memory of a message I had given before, but she sang only two verses and sat down. I was on! The Lord was gracious and I scraped by quite well, but it was scary! I was also asked to preach that evening, but at least I had an hour or two to work on it. For many years after that time, I carried sermon notes in my Bible so I would be prepared for emergencies!

One of the most unusual opportunities I had as a preacher was to dress up in an 1800's costume and preach to some sixty people sitting on hay bales at the newly restored Kline Creek Farm during their annual Harvest Festival, in Winfield, Illinois. (The Kline Creek Farm flourished in the 1890's.) My platform was an old wagon bed and my pulpit was a bale of hay.

I had the privilege of co-officiating at several weddings of former students or of Carol's friends. I was also asked to participate in the ordination of some of our students and graduates, and this was always a special joy. Sometimes I gave the charge (a sermon of challenge) to the newly ordained pastor; at other times, the charge to the congregation to whom the pastor would minister. Over the years, I served on a number of ordination councils, where we would examine a candidate for ordination to the gospel ministry.

B. Sunday School Teaching

Ever since I was in Bible college as a young man, I have taught Sunday school classes whenever the opportunity was given. I had

134

many opportunities while I was on the Moody faculty, and even today I have occasional openings for teaching adult community classes in our church. I love to teach and I accept every chance I get to do so unless it conflicts with other appointments. I have had to turn down opportunities to teach Moody Evening School classes and on-line classes, since they would consume more time and energy than I can now spare from my efforts at writing. My health has been a problem (since 1989 I have had three heart attacks and three strokes). I am grateful to God that I have had no debilitating paralysis!

C. Faculty Bible Lands Tours

One of the most significant sources of academic enrichment, and at the same time, personal stress, came in the form of Moody's Faculty Bible Lands Tours. In exchange for leading or assisting the leader of a tour, full-time Bible Department faculty members were given free airfare with all other expenses paid. The subsidy was financed by the tour price charged other tour members. If enough people were on the tour, the spouses of the two faculty members could also come along free. In addition, faculty members were paid a small stipend for teaching a course while on tour. My wife and I were privileged to go on such a tour of Egypt, Syria, Jordan, Israel, and Greece in 1978. In that tour, I assisted Dr. Alfred Martin. I wrote in my 1978 diary about Egypt: "Cairo is a whole college education in itself! The people, the streets, the quarrelsome officials, the disorganization, the poverty, the dirt and squalor, are breathtaking. And the driving—I was so afraid we would hit pedestrians when our tour bus raced at 60 miles per hour through city streets filled with people. The lanes were ignored. The traffic operates at the mercy of Allah and the horns of the drivers! Police and soldiers are everywhere. We had a bumper collision between the two tour buses. The collision was just laughed off and we went on!" The next day we visited Saqqarah and Memphis, a few miles southwest of Cairo, with their tombs and pyramids. The third day we flew south to Luxor, where we saw several tombs in the Valley of the Kings, Queen Hatshepsut's tomb, and the temple complex at

Karnak. We saw the tombs of the famous King Tutankhamen, Rameses VI, and Seti I. We saw farmers winnowing on the threshing floor in the biblical fashion, women carrying water pots on their heads, and men riding donkeys, each rider holding a stick to prod his donkey on. We toured the Cheops pyramid at Gizah by entering and walking up a ramp to the center, where the marble sarcophagus still rests. It was an exciting experience going up the shaft! I thought of the thousands of slaves who pulled stones up those ramps—stones that weighed many tons—using heavy ropes and wooden pegs. Then we rode camels and had a tour of the Cairo Museum, which is filled with human and animal mummies. We saw the Mohammed Ali Mosque and the Fortress.

Next, we flew to Damascus, Syria. Damascus was extremely interesting, with many bazaars where they sold nuts, spices, rugs, and brass containers of all kinds, most of them turned on crude lathes, with artistic designs. We saw the biblical Street called Straight and the house purported to be that of Ananias, as well as a famous mosque.

From there, we bussed through part of the Fertile Crescent to Amman, Jordan. The Jordanians were friendly and hospitable. We drove down to Petra, the ancient Rose Red City of the Dead, once the capital of Edom, 185 miles south of Amman. Much of the route was desert, affording us a good opportunity to see how the Bedouins live in their black goat hair tents. Camels were abundant, and some Bedouins rode lovely Arabian horses. Petra was just as impressive as the pictures I had seen of this strange city carved out of the red limestone of the mountainside!

We entered Israel through a high security checkpoint at the Allenby Bridge. This made me feel rather uncomfortable and brought home the extreme tension between the Israelis and their neighbors, and between Israel and the occupied Palestinians. I felt the great stress of being in a strange country where I could not speak the language and did not know the customs. Once, while crossing a street in Jerusalem, a taxicab surprised me by driving right in front of my path. I was so frightened, I jumped high into the air! I was so paranoid of the dangers in Israel that Carol thought I was losing my sanity!

We took a cable car to the top of Masada (Herod's ancient fortress). We saw the Old Testament and Roman ruins of Jericho, as well as the modern city of Jericho. We saw Elisha's spring, and Qumran, where a Jewish sect (possibly the Essenes) lived, worked, and worshipped. We saw the caves where the Dead Sea Scrolls were discovered.

In Jerusalem, we toured the house of Caiaphas, David's traditional tomb, The House of the Scroll (Shrine of the Book), containing the Isaiah text from Qumran, and the Holy Land Hotel's model of the city in the time of Herod. On Sunday, we had the thrill of worshipping at the Garden Tomb, just a 10-minute walk from our hotel! We also visited the 14 stations of the cross in the Old City, and the Church of the Holy Sepulcher, with its total confusion of Roman Catholic, Greek Orthodox, Armenian, Coptic, Syrian, and Abyssinian Churches within one building complex. I think the archaeological and historical evidence favors the Church of the Holy Sepulcher as the authentic site of Jesus' entombment. We visited the Mount of Olives east of Old Jerusalem, Gethsemane, where Jesus prayed, the Wailing Wall (the western wall of the temple that dates to Herod the Great), and excavations to the north of the wall that have uncovered some of Solomon's temple foundations! We went through the Dome of the Rock, which caps Mt. Moriah, and saw the Pool of Bethesda where in the biblical account Jesus healed an invalid of 38 years.

At Hebron, we saw the mosque over the Cave of Machpelah, where Abraham, Isaac, and Jacob are buried, along with Sarah, Rebekah, and Leah. We climbed the Herodium, where Josephus says Herod the Great is entombed. (Josephus was a Jewish historian who was born shortly after Jesus' death into a priestly family in Jerusalem.) We visited the open-air market at Beersheba, in the occupied territories of Palestine. We went to the Valley of Elah where David and Goliath fought (1 Samuel 21:9). One of the tour's highlights was to walk through Hezekiah's Tunnel, which Hezekiah's engineers dug to bring water into Jerusalem when it was under siege by the Assyrians, in the late 8th century, B.C.

We also toured Samaria and Galilee. Samaria especially seemed dangerous, as an Israeli sharpshooter soldier was standing atop a church sanctuary to guard our approach to Jacob's well. We were instructed to run to the well, and run back to the bus. We drank from Jacob's Well, and saw the ruins of Ahab's palace in the ancient city of Samaria.

In Galilee, we rode a boat from Teverya (Tiberius) to Kefar Nehum (Capernaum). I preached to our group at the Mount of the Beatitudes. We sat in the courtyard of a beautiful church and were shaded from the hot sun by refreshing trees and the breeze from the Mediterranean Sea. Further north, we saw Baniyas (Caesarea Philippi) where Peter confessed Christ's deity and where the River Jordan begins it southward flow from underground springs fed by the melting snows of Mt. Hermon. Israeli soldiers were cooling themselves in a pool filled by the River Jordan. The bus driver kept in close touch with the military and the Israeli government authorities by radio, and occasionally had to make changes in the itinerary where there was unusual tension with the Palestinians. We could not forget that ancient Palestine was a land largely occupied by Israel, and that there was a feeling of unease and military readiness everywhere. We spent the night at a kibbutz. Facilities were simple but orderly, and all of the residents had jobs to perform and worked hard in a farm setting. They were friendly, however, and seemed content to live in a communal arrangement. The food was excellent and plentiful. There was no evidence of the military at the kibbutz. We visited Cana, where Jesus performed his first miracle, and saw the Church of the Annunciation at Nazareth. This is the supposed site where the angel announced the coming birth of Jesus. (Unfortunately, there are two Churches of the Annunciation.) We stopped at the Plains of Esdraelon and Tel Megiddo, where the Bible predicts that the Battle of Armageddon will be fought. We saw the fascinating ruins of Caesarea Maritima, headquarters of the Roman government in Palestine at the time of Christ.

Flying to Greece, we saw Athens and Corinth. In Athens we climbed the Aereopagus (a low hill northwest of the Acropolis) and saw the agora (the open air market) below. We also climbed the Acropolis and saw the beautiful Parthenon. In ancient Corinth we saw the bema (judgment seat) of Gallio, Apollo's temple, the Acrocorinth, and other things. The Acrocorinth was a mountain to the south of Corinth, where the temple of Aphrodite, goddess of love, once stood.

In July 1988, I had the privilege of accompanying a second Bible Lands Tour, this time as leader. Another faculty member of the Bible Department, Rupert Simms, assisted me. During this second tour, we went to Greece and Israel only. Both tours of Greece included a daylong Aegean cruise. In June 1988, I wrote of this cruise, "The islands looked much the same as ten years ago, except for many more tourists. The water was no longer beautiful blue, but now more greenish (polluted)." As in 1978, each leader taught a course while we were on tour. I taught a course which I had developed, called "Significant Cities in Biblical History." While visiting Masada, Herod's fortress in the south of Israel, one of our tourists, who appeared to be mentally unstable, expressed the desire to commit suicide. Several of us spent hours talking with her and assuring her of God's love and care for her. There are always surprises when touring foreign lands! In Bethlehem, there were police and soldiers everywhere. It was a much more tense atmosphere than in 1978.

One of the highlights of this trip occurred when I climbed a hill near Tiberius and got a beautiful panoramic view of the Sea of Galilee!

In 1994 the annual tour had to be canceled because of violence between the Israelis and the Palestinians. Too few tourists signed up because of their fears.

D. Visiting Foreign Mission Sites

Carol loves maps. We usually had one or two up on the wall. Sometimes it was a map of the United States; other times it was a world map. We also subscribed to the National *Geographic Magazine*, and both our children and we have used it a lot over the years. Carol and I were impressed with friends who took their kids on a short-term mission trip when each was 12. We decided to do the same. We had always had a keen interest in missions, and hoped and prayed that God would lay it on the hearts of some of our children to be missionaries themselves. A short-term trip would expose each of them to peoples, cultures, and climates outside the U.S. and help them focus their attention on the world as a whole.

The first trip was to the nation of St. Lucia, a small island in the eastern Caribbean. I went with Tim when he was 13 and I prepared two courses to teach. One course was for a pastor's convention in

St. Lucia, while the other course was for a children's camp on St. Vincent, a neighboring island. Our missionary friends, the Lehmann's, invited us to come for three weeks. They served under World Team. My first impressions were of the high humidity, heat, rampant poverty, driving on the left side of the road (a British tradition), with steering wheels on the right side of the car, the lack of fans and air conditioning, the intermittent availability of electricity, and the vast differences in diet from what we were used to. It was Sunday, August 3, 1980. I preached that morning, and attended a local pastor's retreat in the afternoon. All that morning and afternoon warnings of a hurricane headed for St. Lucia came over the radio. But the pastors were complacent, saying a hurricane had never hit the island before.

This field work enrichment now promised to be richer than I had bargained for! By 10:00 p.m., the winds were of gale force. By midnight the storm was frightening, with the ceiling of the apartment bobbing up and down, held only by copper wires! Hugo Lehmann and I secured windows and dishes, barricaded the sliding glass doors of the living room that overlooked Castries Harbor, moved furniture, and prepared with candles and flashlights. (The current went off for the last time about 10:00 p.m.) We listened to the battery radio reports as Hurricane Allen struck Barbados and headed straight for St. Lucia and St. Vincent just to the south of us. The eye of the storm was between these two islands as it accelerated to 125 miles per hour, and then headed for the Dominican Republic and Haiti. Between midnight and 1:00 a.m. the five of us (Hugo and Evelyn Lehmann with their son Dan, Tim and I) were huddled on the lower level of my bunk bed in the front bedroom. While we watched, the roof suddenly and rather quietly lifted off and disappeared, letting the rain in! What a strange feeling! Tim and Dan were very frightened, and Evelyn would cry when Hugo had to leave the room to check on a neighbor, Mrs. Richards, and her granddaughter, Sandy, who were invited to stay with us during the storm. The five of us hunkered down on the bunk with nothing but a sheet of plywood from the top bunk above us, while Tim hugged his briefcase with his beloved stamp collection inside! We had only pillows to protect our heads from flying debris. Mrs. Richards and Sandy hunkered under a desk. The floors filled with 1 to 2 inches of water. Papers and small objects were flying about. Shining my flashlight on the trees outside, we could see them bent horizontal with the fierce winds.

About 2:00 a.m., Hugo directed us outside on the side of the apartment away from the wind, as we tried to avoid broken glass, shattered lumber and protruding nails, and then down a stairway to the safer lower level. We heard galvanized steel roofing and other large objects hitting the apartment throughout the night. We brought two foam rubber mattresses down with us and made crude beds for Mrs. Richards and the two children plus Tim, and barricaded the metal louvered window. We sang hymns and prayed and trusted the Lord for his protection.

When it became light again, (about 6:00 a.m.) the hurricane had mostly abated. We went outside to survey the damage. Roofs were missing on about a fourth of the houses in the immediate neighborhood. We later learned that some 14 people were killed in St. Lucia, one of them a man just a quarter of a mile from us, whose house fell in on him. The island suffered widespread damage to houses and trees. All three major crops were destroyed (bananas, mangoes, and breadfruit), so that the island's economy was temporarily ruined. All the electrical poles were down, and no running water was available. Great Britain, Venezuela and the U. S. all helped with food, medicines, temporary housing, and clothing.

After thanking God for sparing our lives, we began cleaning up the mess in the Lehmann's apartment. Debris was everywhere. Many dishes were broken and precious mementos destroyed. I felt very sorry for Evelyn especially, who wept as she went through the house. The sense of loss was very much like the death of a loved one. Hugo had the best theological library on the island, and many books were ruined by the water. We spent a lot of time trying to dry them out. We also hung clothes outdoors to dry and drilled holes in concrete for hooks that would hold more clothes lines. This wasn't what I had planned for our short-term mission trip to St. Lucia, but evidently God wanted to further my missions education!

Another missionary couple, the Ashley's, were gracious to take the five of us in, as their apartment was damaged less severely. I felt sorry for Tim, since his dream vacation in St. Lucia had been shattered! However, he was able to get a flight to St. Vincent and attended a church camp there for the weekend. We moved all salvageable items out of Hugo's apartment and stored them in three different locations. Carol learned, with the help of World Team in Miami, that Tim and I were safe and staying at the Ashley's. Miraculously, Carol was able to call us on the telephone the day after the storm.

We transferred to Peter Rakai's over-the-store apartment in downtown Castries for the rest of our stay. The next two Sundays, I was invited to preach in two different churches. I had no sermon notes with me, and so was obliged to reproduce notes from memory for some of my best sermons. The two courses I so diligently prepared have never been taught to this day! I brought some 70 overhead transparencies for one of the courses, and all the cardboard frames got soaked from the hurricane. When I brought them back to Moody's Audio-Visual Department, I was feeling quite ashamed of the damage. Some of the transparencies had to be replaced; most required new frames. One course was prepared for pastors, the other for children in the camp that was cancelled. Pastors were very busy tending their people and helping those whose houses were damaged by the storm. One church sanctuary was completely destroyed.

Tim and I had some free time and we shopped, swam, snorkeled, and played Frisbee. (We brought a Frisbee to St. Lucia, and kids gathered 'round to enjoy this sport with us.) We also visited the public library, the post office to buy St. Lucian stamps, and a bookstore to browse. One day we tried to climb Gros Piton, the highest mountain on the island. Hugo, Tim and I were with a guide. But the hurricane had covered the trail, and fallen trees and other debris were everywhere. So we were climbing almost straight up, and we gave up after going halfway to the top. It was the hardest climb of my life! We had only a quart of water between us, and Tim began to dehydrate.

We drove clear to the other end of the island to catch our plane home. But when we arrived, the plane had already taken off! So we caught the plane that flew the next day. St. Lucia was an adventure, indeed!

When each of the girls reached 12, Carol took them on short-term mission trips also. Ruth went to the Bahamas. She remembers enjoying the beautiful flowers and trees and gardens. She also distinctly remembers going to a little church where all of the younger children wanted to touch her, especially her hair, since they rarely got a close up look at a white girl. One thing that stands out in Ruth's mind was the huge distinction between the poverty of many of the nationals and the ritzy look of all the tourist hotels and casinos. Ruth loved brushing the hosts' Collie dogs. She was amazed at the coming of the locusts that rained down on the house like hailstones. Meanwhile, Carol taught a communication class at the Daystar Bible College while in the Bahamas.

Joy journeyed to Jamaica. She was in the sixth grade, and she got to take some time off in December before the Christmas break. Carol and Joy stayed two weeks with the Las Neumann family, who was director for the International Fellowship of Christian Students in Kingston. Las's wife was having her second baby, so Joy's main task was to baby-sit Minka, their 2 year-old daughter. Carol and Joy had little time to relax at the beach.

In my opinion, the value of these trips for inspiration, insights into missionary life, and education is beyond calculation. Our daughter, Ruth, along with her family, is a full-time missionary in Spain. Joy has been on missions trips to the Czech Republic, Haiti, the Congo, and France. In 2001, Joy led a group of high schoolers on a short-term mission to—Jamaica!

E. Writing

Since my early years at Moody, I have desired to write books that could benefit others, especially, students. But my heavy teaching schedule and my perfectionism have hindered my productivity in this area. In 1973, I wrote a teacher's manual on unorthodox religious groups. It was titled *The Cults Exposed*, and was published by Moody Correspondence School and used for courses in distance learning.

The "Metheneutics" notes evolved into a book of excessive length, which we have had difficulty publishing because of its extended size. I did a lot of writing on it in 1980-81. It went through a thorough revision and enlargement in 1997 and 1998, becoming a manuscript of over 700 pages! Since then, it has been condensed three times! A possible title is *Getting a Focus on God's Word: An Introduction to the Principles and Procedures of Biblical Interprettion.* As explained earlier, it attempts to integrate two fields that were formerly separated. Hermeneutics deals with how to interpret accurately, and Bible study methods or direct Bible study refers to "inductive" Bible study. Inductive Bible study is a term referring to methods of studying the Bible text itself and learning everything possible from it before using other supplementary helps. My sabbatical in the spring of 1992 allowed me to do further research and writing on this book. We are currently condensing and simplifying the material further so that it will be as user-friendly as possible.

In 1988, Moody Correspondence School published my book, *Elements of Bible Study* for use in courses offered to distance learners. It is still being used by Moody's Distance Learning program on the Internet.

CHAPTER 11
STUDENT ACTIVITIES AND MBI TRADITIONS

One Saturday morning during the summer, I went to the campus to get a cheap haircut offered by a student who was also a barber. The Institute provided him a little cubbyhole where he cut the hair of students and employees by appointment. That day I also watched the male students' annual water fight, sponsored by the Dean of Student's office. The men dressed in swimsuits and grubbies, went out onto Institute Place, and loaded their buckets with water from an old fire hydrant. It had some hilarious episodes and lasted about two hours. Assistant-Dean Mortenson was right in the middle of it with his red trousers! Many of the students watched from nearby, and some of the observers got wet, too!

Another student tradition that I enjoyed was the Women's Open House in Houghton Hall. (Normally Houghton Hall was off-limits to male visitors.) The Open House was held on a Saturday in the fall, and each floor would decorate its rooms and lounge areas to fit a theme. There was a contest to see which floor had the best decorations. Many faculty, male students, and employees would visit the women's dorm on this one day of the year when it was permitted. Later, the men got into the act by having their own Men's Open House in the winter. The students would provide candy and cookies in their rooms. Our children loved to participate in Open House, as did the families of other faculty and employees. One of the big attractions for the children was collecting the free candy and cookies. Since the Women's Open House was near Halloween, our kids were delighted to go trick-or-treating from room to room! The students enjoyed seeing little people around the Institute.

When new resident assistants ("R.A.'s") were chosen, the R.A. for each floor had to wear a silly costume to class for one day, a costume chosen by their floor mates. Some examples I witnessed include Rumple Stiltskin, the wizard of Oz, Jack-in-the-Beanstock, and other well-known fictitious characters.

On May 19, 1971, the students put on a very special extended chapel to honor President William Culbertson for his "godly example and guidance." They did a very memorable job of a "This is Your Life" type of program that reviewed highlights of Dr. Culbertson's life while he was still living, and brought together some of his close friends to express their esteem for the president of Moody Bible Institute. Ten years later, a similar "This is Your Life" chapel was held to honor Dr. Sweeting on his tenth anniversary as president. His wife, Hilda, two of his four boys, his brother (Pastor Norman Sweeting), and his pastor of 56 years, Dr. Braun, were all present. Dirk Van Dam, director of Moody Aviation, piloted a plane that brought the board of Moody Keswick up from Florida. (Moody Keswick was a K-12 school and conference grounds that was given to MBI by the Keswick Foundation.) It was a joyous occasion.

For many years the Junior-Senior Banquet was free to faculty members. The juniors at Moody would sponsor the seniors, inviting them to a banquet in the spring. The juniors were charged a fee to make this event possible. At first a rather modest production held on campus, it gradually grew in glamour and popularity, and, beginning in 1973, was held in some of Chicago's great hotels. It was a lovely occasion, with couples dressed in evening gowns and suits or tuxedos. The dinner was special, and the program was usually inspirational. It often included vocal music by outside groups or soloists, and sometimes a talk by a notable speaker in Christian circles.

Over the years, I attended quite a few senior recitals. They were by invitation from Carol's friends or from my students. These recitals were the climax of a student's music major, and young musicians expressed much appreciation for our attendance. The recitals were formal occasions and they ended with a reception where refreshments were served.

The Music Department required men and women students in the choirs to go on musical tours during the Christmas break, spring break, and sometimes in the summer as well. They did a great job of singing in churches and public auditoriums. The music students gave frequent public testimonies to their faith in Christ, and also shared the Good News with their hosts who took them into their homes. (Some of the hosts were Christians and some were not.) Although the music tours were quite enervating to students who were already tired, they were very beneficial to the churches and other appreciative audiences. They were great publicity for the Moody Bible Institute, an outlet for Christian ministry for the music students, and a way to gain practical concert experience.

Two other musical traditions were the music students' annual presentation of Handel's "The Messiah," often sung in November; and the famous "Candlelight Carols" concert, consisting of Christmas carols, drama, and candlelight presented by all of Moody's choral groups. It was originally held in Torrey-Gray Auditorium, and later at the Moody Church in early December, where it is still held today. In 1986, I remarked in my diary, "Candlelight Carols was exquisite, surpassing our fondest hopes. What a worshipful experience!"

The President's Dinner for graduating seniors was held in the spring each year. These seniors, their parents, and faculty members were invited to this special occasion. The President addressed the seniors, and a few seniors would give testimony to God's blessing on their work at Moody and share their future plans. It was a time to be grateful for what God had done. The Commencement Concert was sponsored by the Music Department, and the best graduating musicians performed spirited music for all who came.

Graduating seniors also put on Class Day exercises. At first, these were held on the same day as spring Commencement, but later they were moved to an earlier day in Commencement week. There were instrumental and vocal solos by some of the top graduating music students, a class song composed by a music major, and speeches given by seniors who were chosen by their classmates. I always enjoyed the Class Day program more than the Commencement itself, since the former offered such variety and gave graduating seniors the opportunity to open their hearts to the entire Moody community.

Of course, the graduation exercises themselves were special too, and we faculty were proud to have a part in thrusting these young people forth into the world to serve our Lord. Some seniors were brilliant, while others graduated by the grace of God and the skin of their teeth, but we loved them all! Some became pastors, some missionaries, some chaplains, and others members of parachurch organizations. Some became evangelists, and some, Christian lay people who would make a difference in their churches. Many would go to graduate school to further their education. Some would go into so-called "secular work," but we believed that if they used what they received at Moody, they would do God's work and accomplish his will, no matter what vocation they followed.

In the fall, I frequently participated in the Reception for New Students, greeting them and often, their parents, who brought them to Moody from all over the country and even from foreign lands. It was stimulating to see how excited they were as they looked forward to their first semester of college. I often wished that they could retain that same exuberance for three or four years! Somehow, college classes, homework assignments, required activities, part-time work, and social activities, along with insufficient sleep, had a way of wearing students down and taking the edge off their enthusiasm. Getting through Moody was hard work. It required a great deal of self-discipline and sometimes, personal sacrifice. It was easy to get discouraged and give up the battle. Likewise, when students from any year came the first day to their new classes, as my diary noted, "Everyone was bright-eyed and bushytailed; would it could be so the whole semester!"

What we shall charitably call an "unscheduled student activity" happened near the end of the spring semester, 1971. A group of students carried a married student's Volkswagon "Bug" into Torrey-Gray Auditorium and deposited it on the platform! It was an elaborate prank, and was removed just in time for a patriotic assembly to be held that honored MBI alumni who had died while in military service to our country!

During my later years of ministry, perhaps in the mid 1980's, The Taste of Moody was born. It was a coming together on one day a year of a group of caterers and food companies to introduce new menus to Moody's cafeteria. The students would freely sample any foods they wanted, and later vote on the ones they liked best. It was a method of advertising, but it also helped to improve the fare available in the cafeteria. The cafeteria made an effort to better its offerings from year to year. In the 60's, when I first came to MBI, the food service was family style, but cafeteria service was soon needed, given the growing student body and the increase in the number of mid-day courses. A single mealtime could no longer accommodate the entire student population.

CHAPTER 12
REGULAR EDUCATIONAL AND INSPIRATIONAL EVENTS AT MOODY

A. Chapel Services

It was a great thrill to hear the students sing, "Great is Thy Faithfulness" at the opening chapel of the school year. It has become a tradition to sing this hymn in Torrey-Gray Auditorium at the start of each semester. I have been moved deeply by it every time. Surely God has been faithful to thousands of Moody students, members of faculty, and all of the Moody Bible Institute family! William M. Runyan, who was affiliated with Moody Bible Institute for a number of years, wrote the tune for this hymn.

One of the nice things about living in the Chicago area is that, eventually, all one's friends seem to visit Chicago for business or pleasure. This makes it possible to renew friendships and keep up with acquaintances more often than in most parts of the United States. I was pleasantly surprised to see, over the years, many evangelicals I had known in Southern California, since they had come to Moody and to Chicago. When they knew I was teaching at Moody, they would look me up on campus. One of these was Dr. Charles L. Feinberg, who at that time was Dean of Talbot Theological Seminary. Another was Walter Dingfield, a friend from the pastoral staff of the Church of the Open Door. A third was Alonzo Le Vert, longtime

President of the Los Angeles Bible Training School. And there were many others.

November 13, 1973 was a special day at Moody. The famous gospel soloist, George Beverly Shea, sang in chapel, and evangelist Billy Graham spoke on communicating the gospel. The same day, the businessman who supplied furniture to the renovated Smith Hall, received Jesus Christ as Savior and Lord. President Sweeting told about it in chapel and we all rejoiced! All of this occurred during a week of special chapels led by Dr. Charles Ryrie, editor of the famous *Ryrie Study Bible.* Among other topics, Dr. Ryrie talked about our responsibility for moral failures, and about asking forgiveness and making restitution.

Chapel services and assemblies were held five days a week. Students were required to attend all of these, and faculty members, several at first. Later, the absolute requirement for faculty was attendance at the President's Chapel on Mondays. On these days, the president or someone he chose would preach a message especially geared to the student body. We were encouraged to attend as many of the other chapels as possible. In September 1987, our administration announced that faculty members were required to attend at least three chapels per week. Many faculty members were unhappy about this, since they were already overscheduled. The requirement was rescinded a few days later, after a special faculty meeting was held to discuss the issue. At first the chapels were only 25 minutes long. Later, they were increased to 40 or 45 minutes to nurture a spirit of worship. Most of the chapels were well planned and spiritually refreshing. Again, some of the best-known speakers in the nation participated. Because of the many pressures on students' time schedules, a few students would read assignments or write letters during chapels or assemblies, but most gave their full attention to the service.

In a Monday chapel in 1984, I had the special privilege of hearing a Christian actor who impersonated Dwight L. Moody. He preached one of Moody's famous sermons on Pontius Pilate. In addition, John Wesley White gave an excellent account of Moody's evangelistic campaigns in Great Britain in an extended chapel during 1986.

It was also very special when Theodore Epp, founder and radio teacher on Back to the Bible Broadcast, shared with the student body some lessons on faith and what God had taught him during fifty years of ministry. That September day in 1985, he announced that he expected this to be his last public appearance, as he was around 80 years old. He went to be with his Lord just a little later the same year.

A unique treat was the opportunity to hear from John W. Peterson in a 1986 chapel. Peterson, who attended MBI, wrote many popular gospel songs. Among them are "It Took a Miracle," "Heaven Came Down," "So Send I You," "Shepherd of Love," and "Jesus is the Friend of Sinners." I noted in my diary, "He's a very ordinary, tall, middle American from conservative Kansas." It's neat that God uses ordinary people!

It was the custom for the dean of faculty or our president to invite faculty members to speak in the chapel at least once during their teaching career. I was privileged to address the entire student body several times during my ministry at Moody. During our first year of marriage, Carol and I sat together in chapel. I was a faculty member and she was in her third year as a student. The faculty colleagues who observed us sitting together would smile among themselves, but they took it in stride.

B. Employee Assemblies

Not only were faculty members expected to attend chapels, but also employee assemblies, which were held once or twice a month in Alumni Auditorium. They were geared mostly for hourly wage workers. They were partly inspirational, but occasionally also included information helpful to faculty about the administration's future plans. Sometimes the faculty members felt overburdened by so many required meetings, and skipped employee assemblies.

C. Missions Conference

The annual fall missions conference at Moody is an intensive three days when regular classes are suspended. All students and faculty are required to attend. Faculty members introduce missionary speakers and assist them in various ways. Sometimes faculty members are asked to chair panel discussions or moderate question and answer sessions. It is a time of learning about mission fields around the world, and a time of vision building. Several mission representatives have told me that Moody's missions conference is their favorite conference on missions, because the students are open to God's leading in their lives and the conference is so well organized. I continue to be impressed that many of our graduates become missionaries, and often return to the missionary conference as speakers and discussion leaders.

D. Founder's Week

Founder's Day (and later, Founder's Week) at Moody was an old and good tradition that dates back to 1901, soon after D. L. Moody's death. It began as a fun day to help celebrate Mr. Moody's birthday, which is on February 5. On the first Founder's Day, the students enjoyed sledding through the snow. By 1919 it had developed into a full Bible conference, where some of the best preachers in the United States (and sometimes, abroad) came for five days and expounded on the Word of God [De Remer, 45-46; Gene A. Getz, *MBI: The Story of Moody Bible Institute*, revised by James M. Vincent (Chicago: Moody Press, 1986), 159.] Students and faculty were required to attend a significant portion of the meetings. It was intended to be a time of spiritual refreshment for all, and a time when alumni and other friends of the Institute came to be encouraged and uplifted. During this week it was always a thrill to see friends and former students whom I had not seen in years. Weatherwise, it is one of the worst parts of the year, but the good preaching and the warmth of renewed friendships made up for it. In my diary I remarked about Founder's Week in 1973: "I attended two fine messages given by Stuart Briscoe and Howard Hendricks. I'm very pleased with the fine spirit of the meetings this year and the positive attitudes of students and faculty." In 1976, I noted that Luis Palau was an excellent speaker at Founder's Week. In his wild gesturing he knocked the water pitcher off the pulpit! Carol and I attended Alumni Day at Founder's Week, 1986, and enjoyed visiting with friends who knew Carol and me and had graduated 20 years earlier.

Moody Aviation had a similar week, called Little Founder's Week. I was privileged to teach at Little Founder's Week in Elizabethton, Tennessee in 1981. Carol and I flew down in a small plane brought up for the purpose, landing at DuPage Airport in West Chicago. Our dean of education, Kenneth Hanna, and his wife, Mary, accompanied us. One of the Moody Aviation instructors capably piloted our 6-seater Beechcraft. Once we were off, it struck me that in my haste to pack, I had forgotten to take any shirts or neckties! Thankfully, Ken Hanna graciously loaned me two of his shirts and a tie. (He wore my exact shirt size!) Ken and I had two sessions each in the mornings, with afternoons free to tour. We got acquainted with quite a few Moody Aviation faculty members, as well as some of the students. We attended a Sweetheart banquet at Milligan College that was held for the Moody Aviation students. Carol and Mary told of their romances leading up to marriage. I told the story of the tinker and the carpenter in *The Checker Players*, using overhead transparencies to illustrate. Ken gave tips on successful marriages. Another day we took a plane ride from the Elizabethton Airport (where the aviation students practice flying), and flew around Grandfather Mountain and back. What a thrilling experience! We ate out each day with aviation faculty or students. I preached a couple of times. It was a wonderful week to get a feel for what life is like for aviation students and faculty.

E. Pastors' Conference

For many years now, a pastors' conference has been held at Moody around Memorial Day weekend, a few days after Commencement exercises for the Undergraduate School. These conferences feature speakers from influential churches, usually pastors themselves. Some of the Moody faculty members are invited to speak, as are various leaders in the evangelical world. As many as 2,000 pastors have attended these conferences, and they receive encouragement, inspiration, Bible teaching, education in ideas, methods, and procedures. They are greatly blessed by the fellowship of fellow pastors from all over our country and abroad. This conference has been used of God to encourage tired, discouraged pastors to persevere in their ministries, since their labors are not in vain in the Lord! Some pastors come who are ready to quit the ministry, but are inspired to continue after attending the conference.

F. Summer Bible Conferences

Every summer, Moody sponsors Bible conferences in several locations. At one time, as many as twenty-five Bible conferences were held under MBI's sponsorship in one year [Getz, 346]. Gull Lake, Michigan, Winona Lake, Indiana, and St. Petersburg, Florida have been frequent sites. The Florida conference was discontinued when Moody sold its Christian school there. These conferences combined solid Bible teaching and preaching with family vacation times, so there are activities for every age level.

G. Commencements

When I first came to Moody, we had three commencements each year: one at the end of the first semester, and another at the end of the school year for the Day School (now known as the Undergraduate Division). A separate commencement was held for the Evening School graduates. I soon discovered that I could purchase my own cap and gown to avoid rental fees. Unfortunately, I could not a get a mortarboard cap that was small enough for my head, and so it bobbed up and down at every commencement procession. I estimate I participated in about sixty commencements besides my own seven. Sometimes I felt like I had gone to school all my life and never graduated until I retired!

After 1990, the winter commencement was discontinued. Still later, the Evening School commencement was combined with the spring commencement for the Undergraduate Division. To relatives and friends who attend, some commencements may seem boring, especially if the speaker is dull or long-winded and the weather uncomfortably warm or humid. The long list of student's names is read off, and the student parades across the platform to receive a diploma or degree. As a faculty member, I admit to experiencing some boredom in listening to less than dynamic commencement speakers. But I remember other speakers who were refreshing, like Elizabeth Elliott of *Through Gates of Splendor* fame, who gave the address in 1994. The thing that most held our interest as faculty members was the privilege of knowing personally many of the graduates at each commencement.

H. Faculty and Management Retreats

After my first week of teaching in 1963, we had our first faculty retreat at the Methodist Campground in suburban Des Plaines, Illinois. It was a day of spiritual refreshment, making new friends among the faculty in a relaxed atmosphere. Our president, Dr. Culbertson, gave a message, and Dr. Coder, the dean of education, read a paper on "The Meaning of MBI as the West Point of Christian Service." Since this was the explosive '60's, during the Vietnam War era when pacifism was popular, a military model came to be challenged. Eventually the slogan was dropped.

In later years, the faculty retreat was combined with a management retreat. However, this did not work well, since perspectives and needs of management were different from those of faculty. And so we went back to the practice of meeting with faculty and educational administrators only. This has continued now for many years. During the years when the Institute had adequate funds, the faculty retreat was a Friday afternoon, Friday overnight, and Saturday occasion. When the budget was tight, we had a one-day meeting on Saturday, with the overnight omitted. The purpose of the faculty retreat was at first more concerned with workshops (which were never popular with faculty). Later, the retreat became more relaxed, focusing on spiritual and social refreshment, getting acquainted with new faculty members, and taking time to visit with faculty we already knew. The faculty retreat became a delightful occasion to which we looked forward. We usually stayed in a resort hotel within driving distance of Chicago. We had greetings from the president, the dean of education, the academic dean, and an inspirational or educational speaker. When funds were available, many of the flight instructors from Elizabethton, Tennessee, flew to the Du

Page Airport in their own small planes in order to join us. It was good to fellowship with them at least once a year. Good meals were served and we had time and facilities for recreation as well. The 1971 retreat included a hilarious all-faculty "Munich Street Band" which made such a hit that it was repeated another year! (The Munich Street Band mimicked the municipal German street bands that played instruments while they marched in their native attire of colorful leather shirts and shorts.)

I sometimes played tennis or took walks with faculty colleagues during the faculty retreat. A faculty committee planned the retreat each year.

One year (1983) Carol played a joke on me to celebrate my 20 years at Moody Bible Institute. She secretly arranged for Brian York, a former Moody student and a limousine driver for Royal Coach Service, to transport us to and from the faculty retreat! One of my colleagues gasped as she saw us being whisked away in style!

J. Other Official School Events

Moody had a Day of Prayer each semester, when faculty and students alike spent the day praying, confessing their sins, and voicing their prayer requests. Classes were spent in prayer instead of the normal lectures. The students went to their regular class-rooms each hour, and the faculty member in charge led in prayer during that hour. A special prayer chapel was held, with a message on prayer, and students led in prayer from microphones set up throughout the auditorium. These prayer days have always been spiritually refreshing for me. Prayer meetings were held in the evening of the Day of Prayer as well.

Another official event was the faculty reception for new students each fall. The reception was more formal in the early years and less so in later years. It provided a good opportunity to meet the new students, and often their parents as well, and welcome them to Moody. The excitement of the new students in coming to Moody was always heartwarming to me.

At the beginning of each semester, we had a special convocation chapel. At first, faculty members wore regular teaching attire for these occasions, but by 1974, we were asked to wear our academic regalia. On a hot August 26 convocation in 1974, I wrote: "We went through the torment of convocation in robes and had a pleasant reception of the new students."

An awards assembly was held toward the end of each semester to honor students who exemplified excellent leadership, unusually fine Christian character, and/or very high academic performance. Many of the awards were partial financial scholarships to help with student expenses. (Although the Moody Undergraduate Division does not charge tuition, the room and board costs, textbook purchases, and other expenses are still considerable, amounting to several thousand dollars per semester for each student.) I was gratified when some of the award-winning students came from my classes.

Once a semester, extended chapels were held for a week, with an outside speaker invited for a series of messages on a theme. This was often a time of spiritual growth for students and others in the Moody family.

Student athletic events were mostly intramural when I first came to the Institute. Our gymnasium was very small, and funds allotted to athletics were scant. Coach Morris Nelson did the best he could with the resources afforded him. The students had an annual Sports Night each April, for which Moody rented a gymnasium elsewhere in the city. They played basketball, volleyball, rope tug-o-war, and other games. When North Hall (a former Masonic temple) was acquired by Moody and renovated, Sports Night was held there. Carol and I attended some of these fun times, and the students appreciated our supporting them. There was some concern on the part of our top leadership that athletics should not be officially emphasized, since a Bible College was mainly to train students for Christian service. This restrictive stance was moderated gradually over the years, and the athletic program got a great boost when the Solheim Center was constructed in 1990 and dedicated in January 1991. Funds for this magnificent gymnasium were donated by a Christian businessman, Karsten Solheim, who invented the Ping golf club, and whose daughters were students at Moody. The Solheim Center made it possible to play conference games, such as basketball and volleyball, with other Christian schools and some secular schools. We were also able to use the gym for outreach in the surrounding community. Our students supervised many underprivileged kid's groups who were thrilled for the chance to use Moody's gymnasium. This opened the way to share the gospel and to influence these children for Christ. Wrestling, tumbling, racquetball, badminton, and all kinds of exercise machines were incorporated into the Solheim programs, as well as a lovely swimming pool.

Family Night was another annual event when all Moody employees were invited to come together for fun, fellowship, and inspiration. One of the most interesting events was the exhibiting of employee hobbies. We learned a lot about each other in this way. I described a Family Night in 1972 that Carol and I helped to plan: "The thirty-four or so hobby exhibits were splendid and exciting. The exhibitors really enjoyed talking with those who came to see their displays. Everything on the whole went smoothly—the band, Dr. Sweeting's personable chat about his family and his wife's family; Munich [Street Band] slides and the Moody Institute of Science film, . . . the hobbies, the care of children and their entertainment, and the lovely meal in the dining hall, with Dr. Sweeting's closing remarks." The same evening, we enjoyed "Faculty Follies" a hilarious comedy dramatizing the eccentricities of certain faculty members.

CHAPTER 13
MY CHRISTIAN GROWTH

A. Church Membership

Although I did extensive preaching at many different churches, Carol and I felt it important to be active members in a local church and attend whenever possible. We were members of Calvary Memorial Church of Oak Park from 1966 to 1969. We made many wonderful friends there, and had opportunity to teach various Sunday school classes as well. Pastor Robert Gray, an excellent preacher, became a good personal friend. Carol helped with Primary Church on Sunday. We attended prayer meetings on Wednesday nights and Sunday morning and evening services. While members here, we dedicated our first two children (Timothy and Ruth) to the Lord.

From 1970 to 1978, we were members of the Pleasant Hill Community Church in the northwest corner of Wheaton. At Pleasant Hill, we continued our pattern of Sunday morning and evening church attendance and Wednesday evening prayer meeting. I was put in charge of the prayer meeting on a number of occasions. At Pleasant Hill, the Lord provided many opportunities to teach classes, preach, and even serve as chairman of the deacon board for two years. The deacons at Pleasant Hill functioned much like elders at most churches. We not only dealt with temporal affairs, but also with those who needed spiritual counsel, encouragement, direction, and even discipline. As chairman, I prepared the agenda and presided at meetings of the deacon's board. It was a time-consuming job, often requiring four to eight hours a week. Sometimes our work was a joy, like when our church was offered the gift of a farm to be used for a camp ground, and sometimes more solemn, as when we had to discipline three young women who regularly disrupted the worship service. We always gave the office our best effort.

I helped organize Sunday evening panel discussions that met about once a month to discuss current issues. They were successful most of the time! When my college and career Sunday school class for young singles was poorly attended, we began meeting in our home after the evening service. We added refreshments, singing with piano or guitar accompaniment to Christian folk songs, and a prayer and share time as well as a Bible lesson. Occasionally, in nice weather, several of the young people would ride their motorcycles to the meeting. We did this for several years, and got to know our college and career young people quite well. Carol took them to Moody's Sunday Night Sing about once a month.

Carol often helped with Vacation Bible School, nursery, and other ministries at Pleasant Hill Church. I even helped her in the nursery for 2 and 3-year olds quite a few weeks. She sang in the church choir for a year or two. She taught Sunday school classes from time to time. Both Carol and I were members of small care and share discussion groups while at Pleasant Hill. These were times of heart searching, praying for one another, and attempts at total honesty and accountability about our spiritual progress.

I enjoyed singing solos from time to time at both Calvary Memorial Church and Pleasant Hill Community Church. I even had the privilege of singing a solo to the entire student body at a Moody chapel on one occasion. Afterward, one of my former students, Peter Philippi, whose life the Lord had touched in a special way, preached the message.

Church renewal was a vital issue in the U. S. from the mid-sixties to the mid-seventies. Some Christians decided they did not need the church at all! Most knew that the church is essential, but we could not always decide what aspects of church life needed to be renewed, or what renewal would look like when it was achieved! Many books were published on the subject. As a result of the discussion, churches engaged in all sorts of experiments, devised alternative types of services, and presented them as models for others to follow. Finally, most concurred that no single model would work for all churches, but that the important thing was for us Christians to recognize that it is the Holy Spirit who brings renewal to the churches, and that all of us need to be open to constructive change, both individually and corporately. When the smoke cleared, some churches went back to their old ways (sameness, tameness, and lameness), but others were stirred with revival and renewal. One controversial issue was music. Should it be traditional, or contemporary? If traditional, which tradition? If contemporary, what kind of contemporary music? Another closely related issue was the remainder of the worship service. Should the liturgy be elaborate, with the reciting of creeds and prepared prayers? Should it be sacramental? Or should it be informal? Was the Holy Spirit permitted to do anything not listed in the bulletin? Or should a bulletin be used at all?

Still another issue was: which is most important—proclaiming the gospel and helping Christians mature—or social service to the poor and needy? Most churches concluded that both were important, and that the two could not be divorced from one another. After we evangelicals finally got over our reacting to the social gospel in liberalism around 1950, we achieved a better balance in emphasizing the whole gospel for the whole person. This was one of the long-term benefits of the church renewal debate, but we still have a considerable way to go. These matters were of keen interest to Moody students, faculty, and administrators alike.

The Jesus People, USA organization ("JPUSA") was born in the early 70's in Chicago, and many Moody students became involved with the Jesus People by attending their services and assisting them with evangelism and social services. A large number of the Jesus People had been homeless and involved in drugs before their conversion, and emerged from street life in America's major cities. And so, the Jesus People in Chicago bought residential buildings in Uptown and lived cooperatively. Moody enrolled considerable numbers of recent Jesus People converts in its day and evening school programs during the 70's. The more traditional students and the Jesus People students were both challenged through the interchange, but it proved to be a growing experience for both groups.

Moody helped the Jesus People gain a solid understanding of Scripture and the Christian life, and they helped us with their passion for evangelism, their warm, non-defensive ways of relating to people, and their hostility toward social and spiritual rigidity.

From 1978 to the present, we have been members of west suburban Wheaton Bible Church. We have enjoyed the ministry of three different pastors while there, and again have had the privilege of teaching a variety of Sunday school classes and being involved in various ministries. From 1999 to 2004, Carol co-facilitated the Career Transition Workshop, with the goal of helping those recently downsized by their employer, those between jobs, and those who seek a better job. They learned how best to present themselves when seeking new employment. She has also taught Sunday school classes on occasion. Currently she is teaching a women's class, and they are responding warmly. She even taught these women the book of Revelation, which I never had the courage to teach myself, except for one occasion!

B. Progress in the Christian Life

It would be gratifying if our personal sanctification (Christian growth in holiness and maturity) proceeded steadily from the time of our conversion to the time we die and go to be with our Lord. But I admit that my growth in Christ-likeness has been a slow and tortuous path punctured with potholes. Spurts of spiritual growth have often been followed by intervals of dormancy or even decay. I think the difference between growth and quiescence is largely determined by my response when the Holy Spirit deals with me about some biblical imperative. I can either say, "Yes, Lord" or "No, Lord." When I say, "Yes," I grow. When I say "No," I decay.

Carol and I went to three different Marriage Encounter weekends during our 40 years of married life, and we found them to be very helpful in enriching our marriage and in encouraging honest, open communication. We learned to write down our emotional issues, and share with each other how it made us feel when our spouse did certain things or showed certain attitudes. We kept up this journaling for perhaps a year or more after our first Marriage

Encounter, and it helped to free us to be up front with each other. Part of my spiritual growth process has been tied to my gradual maturing in our marriage.

In the late 60's I attended Bill Gothard's "Basic Youth Conflicts" seminar while teaching at Moody. One of his sessions was on restitution, a biblical theme seldom explored by evangelicals. Though I did not and do not agree with all of his concepts, God used Bill Gothard to convince me that there were some things in my past that I needed to make right. For many years I had retained a troubled conscience about three things that I knew were wrong. One was stealing fresh fruit as a boy in grammar school. I habitually rode my bicycle to and from school in eastern Los Angeles County. Along the route were a pomegranate tree and a young peach tree. These were temptations, since I have always loved fruit. At first I picked up pomegranates from the ground, reasoning that they would spoil anyway. Then I picked pomegranates off the tree. Next, I stole peaches from the little peach tree near the road.

Much later, when I attended Talbot Theological Seminary in Los Angeles (now known as Talbot School of Theology), I had to turn in reading reports stating I had completed my collateral reading. Since my reputation and my grades were important to me, I sometimes turned in the report *before* the reading was complete. I always got the reading done, but not always by the date I turned in my report. This was a misrepresentation.

Still later, as one of my requirements for the doctor's degree, I took seven comprehensive exams in theology at Dallas Theological Seminary. The rules required each exam to be taken on campus, and no resources to be used. But since I was a commuting student, I took my comps at home, where I would have access to a typewriter and a quiet environment. I did not use other resources to answer the questions, but I knew I had broken the rule requiring that the work be done on campus. I also took several hours for each exam, rather than the two-hour limit the rules laid down. I did not tell the Registrar's Office what I had done. After all, I reasoned, admitting my deviating from the rules could have cost me my doctorate!

Why do Christians sometimes let sins committed after their conversion shadow them for years before confessing them and making them right? Please do not misunderstand me. I believe that when Christians confess their sins to God, he forgives them—all of them—because Christ died for those sins. First John 1:9 says, "If we [Christians] confess our sins, he is faithful and just and will forgive us our sins and purify us from all unrighteousness." But when we sin against fellow human beings, it hinders our *relationship* with them and disrupts our *fellowship* with God. It hinders our faith, our prayer life, and our usefulness for God.

I think one reason we are reticent to make things right is fear for our own reputation or for the consequences. Other reasons are embarrassment and pride.

I finally decided that my need for God's approval and my usefulness for him were more important than my fears, my embarrassment, and my pride. The owners of the fruit trees were either long since dead or had moved away. So I made an offering to my church to cover the estimated value of the fruit stolen. I wrote the appropriate school officials at Talbot and Dallas and confessed the wrongs I had committed, and asked their forgiveness. I am happy to say that in both cases, the respective school officials graciously forgave the wrongs. I was thrilled, and felt like a great load had been lifted from my back!

I did not anticipate the results of these acts of restitution, but ever since those events, I have been freed up to be myself and express honestly my imperfections to my students, my friends, and my family. Surprisingly, my esteem by others did not suffer, but was enhanced!

To the extent that God has used me in and out of the classroom, I owe much of that usefulness to the determination to be honest before God and others, and restitution was one of the biggest factors in that decision.

CHAPTER 14
OUR ADMINISTRATIVE LEADERS

A. Administrators as Models and Encouragers

Administrative leaders should be models of the mature Christian life and encouragers of the faculty, students, and employees. As a member of faculty, the most important leaders for me have been the president, the dean of education, and the dean of faculty (later termed the academic dean, and now titled Vice President and Dean of the Undergraduate School). In every case, I am thankful to say, my educational leaders at Moody have demonstrated the mature Christian life and the desire to encourage. I have not always agreed with their administrative styles, but such differences are probably inevitable. After all, faculty members are very independent minded, and leaders of evangelical organizations may sometimes be slow to discover democratic procedures!

When I came to MBI, our president was Dr. William Culbertson. He was a dignified and godly leader, with a formal appearance and a warm heart. He was also a gifted biblical scholar and a bishop in his denomination, the Reformed Episcopal Church. He passed away from bone cancer on November 16, 1971 after serving as president for 23 years. A special assembly was held the next day and we were informed of his death. His last words were, "O God, God, yes!" The entire school attended his memorial service in Torrey-Gray Auditorium on November 19, 1971.

Dr. George Sweeting followed Dr. Culbertson in the president's office on September 28, 1971. Dr. Sweeting had pastored the Moody Memorial Church. He also wrote a number of books about the Christian life, and had a fine radio ministry over WMBI and affiliated stations. He was featured as narrator in some of the Moody Institute of Science films. Dr. Sweeting had a flair for chalkboard art, and every two or three years the students would talk him into presenting a chapel where he would draw a picture with colored chalk and illuminate it with ultraviolet light. He would apply the drawing to the Christian life and it was very effective.

In chapel, we celebrated Dr. Sweeting's 60th birthday on October 1, 1984. Sweeting narrated some of his past life, especially the story of his being reduced to 129 pounds through cancer and his providential recovery. He also told us of knocking a drunken man down by accident on the "El" platform, then rescuing him from the "El" tracks! How neat to be able to relate to our president by sharing in stories of his life!

Dr. Sweeting's tenure was followed by Dr. Joseph Stowell, who was inaugurated on September 28, 1987. He was a graduate of Cedarville College and Dallas Theological Seminary. He came as a successful pastor. As a relatively youthful president and a sports fan (especially soccer), he was greatly admired by the students. When Dr. Stowell first came to Moody, he had lunch with about ten students at the Paddyaya Thai Restaurant on Chicago Avenue. Among these students was our son, Tim. When Dr. Stowell asked what improvements could be made at MBI, Tim responded, "Pay the teachers more!" Joseph Stowell was also an excellent speaker and an author. After serving for seventeen years, Dr. Stowell resigned to become a pastor of the Harvest Bible Chapel. All three of these presidents have had an effective outreach in proclaiming God's Word over the Moody Radio Network.

When I first came to Moody, the dean of education was J. Maxwell Coder. He was a close friend of President Culbertson and the two worked well together. At that time it was the custom of the dean of education to preside at faculty meetings. Later, this task was entrusted to the dean of faculty (later called Academic Dean).

Following Dean Coder's term of office, Dr. Alfred Martin became the dean of education. He had already served with distinction as a faculty member, and had then been promoted to the responsibility of dean of faculty. After Dr. Martin retired, Dr. Kenneth Hanna became dean of education. We had a fun birthday party for Dr. Hanna's 50th birthday, complete with "over the hill" hardware such as denture grip and a toupee. After some years of service, he was followed by Howard Whaley, who had served on the faculty for many years and taught church history with much skill.

The office of academic dean also saw changes. My immediate boss in 1963 was Dr. Alfred Martin. When he became dean of education, the office of academic dean was taken up by Dr. Donald Smith, a faculty member who taught homiletics. Smith was followed by W. Sherrill Babb, who came from Philadelphia College of the Bible. Jay Fernlund, an internal administrative assistant held the office next, followed by Howard Whaley. When Whaley became dean of education, Robert Woodburn took his place as academic dean.

B. Rules

Moody has always been known as an evangelical Protestant school that is non-denominational, but welcomes students from many denominations. The school has also been known for its conservative perspective on both doctrine and lifestyle. While striving to avoid legalism, Moody has nonetheless maintained a rather extensive list of expectations (rules, if you please), for its faculty, its students, and its non-faculty employees. The rules have differed for each of the three groups above. The expectations are in some ways more rigorous for faculty members, who are modeling the Christian life and Christian service while they teach. But faculty members also have some liberties that students do not have. Expectations for other full-time employees of the Institute are similar, but less rigorous. Rules for students take into consideration their relative Christian maturity. The sensitivity of each group's relationship to Moody Bible Institute is considered. (How would each group affect Moody's testimony and reputation to the families, churches, pastors, donors, mission boards, other Christian organizations, and to other schools similar to Moody?) It is impossible to please everyone, but the Institute has tried to require Christian lifestyles that are first, biblical, and secondly, are approved by the vast majority of its constituency. Moody has done fairly well with this, but has not always succeeded in its sensitivity to changing cultures, fairness, and balance. Dress codes have changed over the years, and most of them have allowed more and more freedom of choice. One criticism has been that MBI was too much concerned about others' opinions and was not always consistent with the Bible's teachings on these matters. Occasionally, faculty members were divided in their views of administrative policies. Were they too rigid, not adequately considering cultural changes? Or, were they just right? (Almost no one felt they were too permissive.) Personally, I favored the conservative dress code required of students and faculty in class and around the campus. I felt that it gave all of us a reminder of our seriousness of purpose.

For many years, movies were forbidden for faculty, employees, and students. I was in general agreement with this policy. But students and faculty were both dismayed when our administrators announced in 1974 that we were not allowed to attend the Billy Graham film, "Time to Run," because it was being shown in public theaters. The policy on theater attendance was modified in later years, first for faculty, and then for students. In 1991, after ten years of study and two committees, the administration decided to permit discretional viewing of movies for faculty, but not for students while on campus. During summer vacations, students were allowed to view movies at their parents'discretion.

School policies appropriately reflected Moody's position as a Christian institution that was conservative in doctrine and lifestyle. In the 60's, the dress code consisted of dress slacks, dress jacket, dress shirt and tie for men, and a dress or skirt and blouse for women. Dresses and skirts were not to be much shorter than knee length. Neckties were dispensed with for male students, but not for faculty, beginning in the 70's. During the 60's and 70's, men's hairstyles and length of hair became an issue. Moody had to strive for balance between the very conservative dress code expectations of some of the churches who sent students to us and the non-Christian public we were trying to reach with the good news of the gospel. That balance was often difficult, and sometimes, elusive. I realized that the dress code was based in part on contemporary business dress, and also in part on the conservative constituency who donated funds to MBI.

Dress codes have been modified considerably since the 60's and 70's, but modesty and neatness are still considered important. I feel that Moody's requirements of its faculty, employees, and students were better balanced in 1995 when I left than in 1963, when I began my teaching career there.

C. Administrative Recognition of Faculty

Our administration sponsored a special celebration to commemorate each faculty member's twenty-fifth anniversary of teaching at MBI. A program of recognition was held and refreshments served. The faculty member could decide what form the program would take. For example, some wanted simple speeches; others, readings; still others, skits or movies showing the life of the teacher. A similar celebration was held when the faculty member had served thirty years. A dinner and program were also held at the time of a faculty member's retirement. The faculty member was permitted to invite about 30 guests, including family members, close friends, and colleagues. The administration would present a gift Bible and a plaque honoring the retiree, as well as cash gifts and cards from colleagues. Similar courtesies were also extended to other employees who were not members of faculty.

I was deeply moved by the program celebrating my 25 years at Moody. Carol and all our kids were present. Rosemary Turner and Harold Foos spoke about my character, friendship, and teaching career. Howard Whaley, the current academic dean, said some nice words as well. Carol showed slides of our family and me from 1963 to 1988. I was given a monetary gift to buy a much-needed brief case, and signed cards were presented as well. Our family ate lunch together in the Coffee Cove.

My thirtieth anniversary of teaching was also recognized with a party. My family members and quite a few faculty colleagues were in attendance. Our daughter Joy, with help from Carol and Ruth, did a hilarious skit highlighting a few of my many eccentricities. It was called "A Day in the Life of Dr. Nevin." Joy wore one of my suits and my straw hat, and she did a great job of acting! Each of our three children said a few words of appreciation about their dad, and I was emotionally touched by it.

Another recognition of one faculty member each year came through the administration's Alumni Association. On February 2, 1982, I was about to take a nap when Carol, who had come in to MBI to attend the Alumni Day and banquet at Founder's Week, obviously expected me to come with her to the alumni program at 2:30. "Oh well," I thought. "Since she is here, I will accompany her." I had no thoughts of being chosen as the recipient of the Alumni Faculty Citation, but when they started to read the life history of the recipient, he was born November 30, 1932. "Of all things," I remarked to Carol, and then I looked at her. She had a gleam in her eye, and I said, "You rascal!" This award includes a beautiful engraved bronze plaque and $3,000 for professional improvement! What an honor! Carol received six red roses also. She had brought the kids, and they had hidden themselves around the MBI campus all day to stay out of my sight. But when I received the award, they all gathered around me on the platform of Torrey-Gray Auditorium! It was a high point of my entire life! Thank you, Lord, for such an honor to your unworthy servant! With the $3,000 I bought the second personal computer any Moody faculty member had in his or her office! Several other personal computers followed in the years since, and they have helped me tremendously in word processing. This included classroom preparation, papers I did for graduate work, making of exams and quizzes, notes for students to purchase, various writings, Sunday school lesson notes, sermon notes, and many other benefits.

D. Teacher Evaluations

Teacher evaluation was something that I feel was a real weakness at Moody. In theory, department chairpersons were encouraged to evaluate their teachers' performances in the classroom on a regular basis. In practice, however, the chairpersons were heavily loaded with extra responsibilities besides their teaching load, and could seldom carve out enough time to do this. I taught full-time for nine years before a chairperson observed my classroom teaching! The feedback was minimal. In twenty-one years of teaching, I noted in 1984, only three times was one of my classes officially observed to evaluate and improve my teaching. I felt that an assistant to the academic dean should be hired for the specific purpose of assisting faculty members, especially new ones, in improving their classroom teaching styles, giving guidance about student homework loads, grading, etc. But this never came about. We did have a 15-30 minute appointment with the academic dean once a year. He informed us of his overall evaluation of our performance, and shared the amount of our salary increase when an increase was approved.

E. "Them" and "Us"

It is most regrettable when faculty members and administrators to whom faculty are responsible do not adequately communicate with each other. This causes some mutual trust to erode and tensions to flourish. The result is low faculty morale and misunderstandings on both sides. This "us versus them" mentality undermines unity and harmony and makes everyone's jobs harder than they should be. Such a tension built up at Moody in 1970. Part of the faculty's distress was due to the facts that emerged from our American Association of Bible Colleges self-study for renewed accreditation. Another trigger was a full page *Newsweek* article (March 9, 1970, p. 51) called "The Mood at Moody." While the article said some complementary things, it was mostly critical of MBI. It accused Moody of being racist, of having a military mentality, of neglecting the "decaying neighborhood around it," of being too strict in lifestyle standards, and of considering rock music a tool of the devil. Many in the faculty felt that our administrators did not adequately answer the article. A third factor was that some professors felt badly overworked and undervalued, and a few decided to leave as soon as they could secure teaching positions elsewhere.

Also in 1970, Richard Mohline, Dean of Students, was accused of insubordination and asked to resign. He was well liked by faculty and students alike, and this was a discouragement to many. Tensions came to a head when I and several other faculty members decided to draft a letter requesting a special meeting of the faculty to discuss serious morale concerns and the communications gap between faculty and administration. I circulated this letter for signatures from concerned faculty. The administration learned that I was circulating a petition among the faculty, and this seemed to some administrators to be an act of subversion. My position hung in the balance for a week or more, but, to their credit, the administration did honor faculty's request for a special faculty meeting. Unfortunately, the school year was about to end, so the only day we could meet was Commencement Day on June 5, 1970. While we would ordinarily be congratulating students upon their graduation, we were in a very intense faculty meeting! In the meeting, I tried to reassure our administrators that we were for them, not against them, and that this was not a revolt, but a serious appeal for better communication. I kept my composure, but I was inwardly afraid and emotionally distraught as I read the preliminary report of my sub-committee on the AABC self-study that included the results of a faculty questionnaire. Then, some half-dozen of the most concerned faculty members spoke of the need for a sympathetic listening ear among our administrators. Although no action was taken at this meeting, a channel of communication was opened which gradually improved faculty morale.

This was also the year when many colleges and universities closed temporarily during the spring semester due to student protests and student riots. Some of the protests were touched off over President Nixon's decision to send American troops into Cambodia; others were protests over a tragedy at Kent State University in Ohio. Students at Kent State demonstrated against the Vietnam War, and the Ohio National Guard fired upon the demonstrators. Four students were shot and killed in the attack. The atmosphere throughout our country was tense. A week later, two students were shot and killed by police at Jackson State University in Mississippi. By May 6, 1970, over one hundred American universities and colleges experienced student protests. Among them were the University of Cincinnati in Ohio, Syracuse University in New York, Washington University, St. Louis, Missouri, University of Virginia; University of Kansas; and Valparaiso University in Indiana. The University of Illinois experienced student unrest as well.

In 1973, at the beginning of the fall semester, our administration announced a kind of 10-year plan for the undergraduate division. We faculty members were thrilled that our administrators were willing to share their hopes and dreams with us that dealt with the education branch of the Moody Bible Institute! This event showed tremendous progress in faculty-administration relationships since the darker days of 1970!

Dr. Stanley Gundry was asked to resign in 1979 because he tolerated his wife's views on Christian feminism. This seemed unfair to many faculty members. Out of this incident grew the Grievance Committee designed to protect faculty members from arbitrary dismissal. Dr. Gundry did resign and eventually became Vice President and Editor-in-Chief of the Book Group at Zondervan Publishing House.

In the fall of 1981, the Bible Department learned that our administration wished to cancel the department's Bible Lands Tour for the summer of '82. The reason was that top administrators wanted to run their own tour that summer. The Bible Department sent a strongly worded protest, and our tour was spared.

President Stowell initiated an occasional faculty colloquium, an informal discussion time between faculty members and administration, in April 1991. Some mutually beneficial airing of issues resulted, and brought administrators and faculty into a closer understanding of one another, resulting in a greater sense of working together.

CHAPTER 15
MOODY'S INSTITUTIONAL DEVELOPMENT

A. Undergraduate School

When I first came to Moody in 1963, we had a three-year curriculum with a diploma presented upon graduation. In 1965, the three-two plan began with a B. A. degree in Bible/Theology granted after two years at another college or university. The American Association of Bible Colleges originally accredited this B. A. degree.

The first Theological Lectureship, sponsored by the theology department, began in November 1968. Clark Pinnock was the first guest lecturer. The Theological Lectureship consisted of a one-hour morning chapel, followed by a one-hour evening lecture the same day. The lectureship became a tradition and continued in subsequent years.

In 1970, The Missionary Technology Department was split into the Missionary Aviation Department and the Missionary Radio Department, with faculty status granted to all full-time instructors.

The school year calendar was changed in 1971, partly to avoid "lame duck sessions" of one week of classes after Christmas vacation before the fall semester ended. Before the change, our school year began in mid-September and ran until mid-June. After the changeover, we began the fall semester the last week in August and ended the spring semester in mid-May. This change proved to be a great improvement. We not only avoided splitting up the fall semester, but we also made it possible for students to get better summer jobs before the job market was full.

After much debate and study, in 1977, Moody's faculty accepted a statement explaining our philosophy of education. I was not fully satisfied with it, since it seemed to emphasize academics more strongly than spiritual life. This is a continuing deep concern for me at MBI, that we will always have a good balance between academics and the spiritual growth and practical preparation of the students to proclaim and model the message of the gospel.

Also in 1977, faculty ranking was instituted. I was generously given the title of Professor of Bible and Theology. The ranking system was conventional, starting with instructor, then assistant professor, then associate professor, and finally, professor. The ranking standards depended partly upon seniority, partly upon educational attainments, and partly upon reputation for excellence in teaching. I suppose I was given the rank of full professor partly because I had been at Moody for fourteen years, partly because I had a doctorate, and partly because I was considered one of the better teachers. Before ranking was begun, all full-time faculty members were simply called members of faculty. Part-time teachers did not enjoy faculty status.

In 1979, Moody had the largest entering class of freshmen in our history up to that point: 633. The faculty voted to try having a 30-minute break after chapel, before the next class began. This experiment, begun in 1981, worked so well that it was continued permanently.

Moody began to offer its own 4-year B. A. program in 1985. Four years later (1989), the North Central Association of Colleges and Schools accredited Moody's undergraduate program. Following this, an articulation agreement was reached with several local universities by which Moody students could get a year of general education courses at other schools while keeping Moody's three year curriculum intact. This enabled Moody Bible Institute to offer a B. A. degree. Eventually, however, this plan also appeared inadequate. After much soul-searching, it was decided to bring the general education courses on-campus. Today, Moody offers its B. A. degree with all four years taken at Moody Bible Institute. A strong effort has been made to hire Christian professors with specialized training in general education areas who uphold Moody's doctrinal position and world-view. My own feeling was that these moves each represented a stage in our progress toward wider acceptance as a college, and that they were fine, as long as we held firmly to our mission. I was concerned that these changes would not lead to a secularization of the school. To date, I think Moody has been successful in protecting our mission as a <u>Bible</u> Institute. I expressed concern in 1992 that the general education courses might come to overshadow our emphases on Bible, theology, missions, evangelism, and Christian service. I felt that requiring 46 hours in general education would be excessive. But upon reviewing the Moody Undergraduate Catalog of 2004-2006, I noted that the semester hour requirement was 40 rather than 46. I was thrilled to observe that the general education courses are thoroughly imbued with Moody's Christian worldview and properly reflect its special mission in education. They support the rest of our curriculum and I believe the course descriptions will be a model for other Christian schools that struggle with attempting to integrate so-called secular courses with their Christian worldview.

B. Evening School

It was a joy for me to teach in the Evening School. The students were mostly adults in their 30's, 40's or 50's who worked full-time. Some were pastors, while a few were retired, but all were excited about learning more about the Bible in order to sharpen their knowledge and skills in Christian ministries. A few were young people of college age who hoped to be admitted to the Day School by making good grades in the evening program. Many of the Evening School students could barely afford the very modest tuition charged. They would come once or twice (a few, three times) a week in the evening after rushing to school from their jobs. Many of them would do this for five or ten years, so eager were they to learn. They would put what they learned into immediate practice in their churches and communities. They came at great sacrifice and always appreciated what they received. In the 60's, Moody began branching out to other communities with course offerings in Evening School. The Evening School on the Chicago campus was still the largest, but other locations were often successful as well. At different times, I taught Evening School in Wheaton and also in Elgin, but most of my Evening School classes were in Chicago. I would take a late train home. Sometimes my schedule took this into consideration so that I would not have an 8:00 a.m. class the next morning.

One of the most popular Evening School courses I taught was on spiritual gifts. Evening School students came from a wider variety of churches than Day School students did, and this sometimes included charismatic congregations. I noted in my 1974 diary, "Some of the . . . students got carried away [became very emotionally expressive] as I spoke about the gift of prophecy. We nearly had a holy riot!"

Today, the Evening School has broadened into what is now called the Extension Studies Program. There are four locations in northeastern Illinois, including the Chicago campus; two in Indiana; one in Spokane, Washington (includes both day and evening programs); about a dozen locations in Ohio, and some seven locations in Florida. Many of these courses offer college credit and are fully accredited.

C. Correspondence School

The Correspondence School was a thriving enterprise when I came to Moody in 1963. Since then, it has evolved into External Studies, and finally into the Distance Learning Center. Moody has one of the largest correspondence programs in Christian schools in America. It has long reached into America's prisons to evangelize, encourage, and teach those who are incarcerated. Both individuals and groups of lay Christians have studied Moody correspondence courses that have greatly enhanced their knowledge of the Bible, Christian doctrine, evangelism, missions, the Christian life, and the Christian home. At first, these courses were accredited by the Correspondence School only, but they gradually increased in their sophistication and levels of learning. Moody's Evening School came to give credit for some correspondence courses. Later, college level courses were developed, and students from Moody and other Christian schools were allowed college credit toward their graduation from some of the correspondence courses. The Correspondence School had its own staff of instructors who graded papers and gave personal attention to students who sent in their questions. These instructors were supplemented by Undergraduate faculty and sometimes by their wives, who were given moderate payments for correcting papers.

Today, The Distance Learning Center offers not only correspondence courses by mail, but on-line courses as well. It also has regional classroom instruction in several parts of the country. Both on-line courses and print courses are fully accredited. What used to be called the Correspondence School is now called Independent Studies. The Independent Studies Program offers both Bachelor's and Associate degrees. It is "one of the oldest and most respected study-by-mail schools in the world." [Quoted from the Distance Learning website of www.moody.edu]

D. Radio Ministry

Very few schools have their own radio station, let alone a network of radio stations. One of the truly special opportunities that many faculty members have enjoyed is to speak on WMBI and its affiliated stations. I declined some of these opportunities, but one invitation I did accept was to give a series of twenty-four fifteen-minute addresses on basic Bible doctrine. I also taught Principles for Interpreting the Bible on the radio. I spoke on a number of other radio programs over the years, but seldom as a series.

Moody Radio began in 1926, when many Christians thought radio was of the devil because Satan was called in the Bible "the prince of the power of the air" (Eph. 2:2, KJV). Radio Station WMBI was the first religious radio station in the nation. Today, the Moody Radio Network owns and operates over thirty radio stations across the United States. WMBI is also available on the Internet and through satellite connections. It truly has a global voice for God.

E. Graduate School

The Moody Graduate School opened in 1985. Although I did not have the privilege of teaching there, graduate students have been very excited about their courses and professors. One of the reasons for this is that many classes were offered through team teaching by one theorist and one practitioner. (A theorist is a teacher who is familiar with the biblical basis, philosophy, and logical analysis of the subject; a practitioner is a teacher who has had field experience in the subject he is teaching, such as pastoral ministry, discipling, or evangelism.) This has resulted in a good balance between academics and practicality. There are two types of arrangements: (1) resident students, who take courses in regular semesters, and (2) module students, who come for 2 weeks at a time of intensive study, preceded and followed by assigned reading, papers, and other projects. The module plan makes it possible for students already in vocational positions to attend without serious disruption to their ministries.

I never heard any graduate students complain about their courses or professors. This is unusual and very commendable! After the Graduate School was born, the Day School was renamed the Undergraduate Division. Our own daughter, Ruth, attended the Graduate School for three semesters and enjoyed her classes immensely. A few of our Undergraduate professors permanently transferred to the Graduate School and no longer taught in the Undergraduate Division. Additional faculty members for the Graduate School were hired from the outside.

The Graduate School first offered an M. A. degree, with the first six graduates receiving that degree in May 1988. Although the Undergraduate Division was accredited by the North Central Association earlier, a few years later the Graduate School was also awarded accreditation. In recent years, a Master of Divinity degree has been added for a seminary track.

F. Diversity at Moody

Every few years, an article about Moody would appear in Chicago's news media. Reporters would usually compliment the school for remaining in the city when other schools fled to the suburbs, but occasionally they criticized MBI for being too strict in lifestyle rules and for being racist. The most severe criticism that I am aware of appeared in *Newsweek* for March 9, 1970. *Newsweek* noted that, during Founder's Week of 1970, a public demonstration was held by "a handful of black Moody graduates against the school's 'institutional white racism.'" In front of TV cameras, "Moody alumnus Melvin Warren shredded his diploma into a trash can while Leona Jenkins, another Moody graduate, held aloft a sign: 'Woe unto you, hypocrites—Luke 11:44.' Moody Bible Institute, Warren charged, bans interracial dating, practices segregation in dorm room assignments and refuses to allow neighborhood children—mainly blacks and Puerto Ricans—to use the school's gym. Furthermore, Warren contended, the administration refuses to allow black students to travel with Moody's globe-trotting choir."

So far as I was able to learn, all of these charges were true in 1970. But since then, every one of these flaws has been corrected. There has been no segregation in dorm room assignments for many years now. Interracial dating is permitted, and our students invite neighborhood kids to use our gym and supervise them in a number of programs held there. Many of our students have befriended the kids who lived in Cabrini-Green, which, until it was torn down in 1993, was one of the most notorious public housing projects in America, just a few blocks west of campus. Our students started project 412, named after 412 W. Chicago Avenue in Cabrini-Green, in 1969. Moody students would knock on doors and ask kids if they wanted to learn about Jesus. This would lead to Bible clubs with the approval of the parents. The program later expanded to include athletic events and scholastic tutoring. Our students filled the roles of big brother and big sister to these kids, ate out with them, played with them, and became real friends. There is no longer any racial discrimination in Moody's touring choral groups either.

We have an increasing number of foreign and minority students in the undergraduate and graduate student body. Moody has always had a very large number of minority students in the evening school program. When I came to Moody, black and Hispanic *employees* were largely limited to the lowest level jobs at Moody. But, in 2001, Dr. Larry Mercer, a black man, was appointed Senior Vice President of Media and Church Ministries. As such, he is part of the seven-member executive cabinet. Also, in 2003, Walter White, Jr., a black graduate of 1978, became executive director of the Moody Alumni Association. After graduating from Moody, Walter had continued his education at the University of Illinois in Chicago, and later had earned his master of theology degree at Dallas Theological Seminary.

G. The Growth of Moody's Campus

When I came to Moody in 1963, the campus consisted of two blocks bounded by Chicago Avenue, Wells Street, Chestnut Street, and La Salle Street (now La Salle Blvd.). There were many small businesses around us, but their buildings were badly deteriorated. The surface of Moody's campus was all concrete, with a few flower boxes constituting the total landscaping. Moody's original building, 153 Institute Place, was still standing. There, D. L. Moody's former office was still intact. The 153 building was demolished during the summer of 1969, to make way for Culbertson Hall, the men's dormitory. Norton Hall was located on the north side of Institute Place, and housed another dormitory, the old Sweet Shop, and a small gymnasium in the basement. Beside it was the Guild Hall, with a nursery upstairs for the children of students' wives. Other buildings on campus included Torrey-Gray Auditorium, Doane Memorial Music Building; Smith Hall, Towner Hall, Crowell Hall, Alumni Auditorium, and Houghton Hall (the women's dormitory). Fitzwater Hall was only a year old in 1963. An underground tunnel system shielded us from the icy blast of Chicago's winter winds, and connected almost every building. My favorite building was Fitzwater Hall, where I spent most of my working hours.

During my ministry at Moody, Norton Hall was demolished and Smith Hall was refurbished. The Coffee Cove in the lower level of

Smith Hall replaced the original Sweet Shop in Norton Hall. A multi-level parking facility was built (1986), the Masonic Temple purchased and partially remodeled as North Hall. In addition, Emma Dryer Hall, located north on La Salle St., was purchased and used as a dormitory. The Solheim Center—a world-class gymnasium—was built, complete with large swimming pool, and dedicated in January 1991. The Morningside Apartment Building, located two blocks north of the campus, is Moody's newest housing acquisition (purchased in 1999). It still houses some senior citizens. Recently renamed Jenkins Hall, It will be used for married undergrads and graduate students. About one-third of the building is now being used for students [*Moody Memo*, January, 2005].

A soccer field was added to the northwest. Several surface parking lots were built and placed into service, and the tunnel system was remodeled and enlarged. (The original tunnel system reminded me of the aisle in a submarine, where I often scraped my head on the ceiling or banged into water pipes sticking out of the wall—and I'm not tall!)

Several other buildings were acquired west of Wells Street for Moody Press administrative offices, *Moody Magazine* administrative offices, and others. New classrooms, faculty offices, and a communications laboratory were added when the Sweeting Center was completed in 1991. The library was then relocated from Crowell Hall to the lower level of the Sweeting Center. Crowell Hall was remodeled to house more up-to-date classrooms and offices, and the WMBI studios were completely rebuilt and new radio equipment purchased. The administrative offices in Crowell Hall were redone as well. The most recent building is the lovely new Alumni Center, just south of Torrey-Gray Auditorium. Today, we have a lovely new Coffee Cove in the Alumni Center.

Moody Press (today known as Moody Publishers) originally had a warehouse on Wells Street, but it became overcrowded with the growth of the Press. They decided to contract with a company that warehoused our books downstate. In 1975 Moody Press experienced a crisis when this company proved unreliable. Consequently, Moody purchased a warehouse in Northbrook, Illinois, where our daughter, Joy, currently resides. They asked for volunteers to help them clean and prepare the used warehouse for storing books, tracts, and other items. Our family put in a hard five hours there on Labor Day, 1975. Joy, aged 2 1/2, prayed over every tract stack that Carol packed, saying, "Thank you for this stack of cards!"

Many other faculty, employees and students helped as well. Since then, Moody Press was able to acquire a more convenient warehouse west of Wells Street that made it easier to bring books and supplies to the campus bookstore.

The maintenance of the campus buildings and landscape at Moody has been a matter of pride and good stewardship. Nevertheless, there were some maintenance issues. The heater/air conditioning system in Fitzwater Hall never did work as well as intended. Each faculty office contained one of these units, and the source of heat was circulating hot water. After Fitzwater Hall had aged to twenty plus years, the units gave a great deal of trouble. For example, the day after Christmas, 1983, I was studying in my 210 Fitzwater Hall office most of the day. I was alone in the building. I smelled steam and investigated. Water was rolling down the hall. A water pipe had broken in the heater unit in 201 Fitzwater Hall. Student employees shut off the water and vacuumed up the mess. Later I discovered that the water had again begun leaking at full force. On another occasion, the water pipe broke on the third floor of Fitzwater, and leaked through the ceiling, ruining a computer. And again, the day after Christmas, 1990, I was about to leave for home when I discovered a plumbing leak that flooded the men's faculty lounge, spread to the third and second floor hallways and seeped through the ceiling tiles of the back stairwells. I alerted the Crowell Hall deskman and he sounded the engineer's alarm. The reception area and academic dean's carpets had to be replaced, and tiles were replaced in the men's faculty lounge as a result of water damage.

In the fall of 1991, Moody's new library was opened to students, faculty, staff, and even to the general public. With its new location in the Sweeting Center, it was much larger than its previous home in Crowell Hall, and much better equipped, with excellent lighting, numerous study carrels, and new book shelves. Before the new library was built, the faculty assisted in discarding outdated materials and in suggesting new materials to be purchased to support the courses each taught. The library budget was increased to allow more expansion of its holdings in light of the enlarging areas of study, the Graduate School's needs, and the fact that general education courses were now being taught in-house.

In April 1992, after 29 years in the same office in Fitzwater Hall, I vacated that cramped space for a new, larger office, # 340, on the third floor of the Sweeting Center. Facing east, from its front windows I could see the business buildings up and down La Salle Boulevard, and some of the high-rise buildings nearer the lake, notably the John Hancock Building. It was a much nicer view than I had in the old office, and I enjoyed new furniture as well. I stayed in the Sweeting Center office until my retirement in 1995. Most of the faculty moved to the Sweeting Center, but some stayed in Fitzwater Hall, and many of the Graduate School faculty remained in Smith Hall.

Today, the Moody campus is four to five times the size of its 1963 campus. Much beautiful landscaping exists today, including trees, grass, flowers, and benches.

To reflect a bit on MBI's earlier campus history, the big pointed arch in Crowell Hall became a symbol of the Moody Bible Institute in 1939 [Timothy R. Wise, "The MBI Logo," in *MBI Memo*, March, 1986, p. 4]. In that year, the arch was formally dedicated during Founder's Week. However, the first graduating class to march in caps and gowns through the arch did so in the previous year [Bernard R. De Remer, *Moody Bible Institute: A Pictorial History* (Chicago: Moody Press, 1960), 84.] The arch "overpowered all of the existing structures and dominated the campus" [Walter Osborn, Reference Librarian at Moody Bible Institute, in an e-mail communication to the author, Oct. 10, 2004]. Moody's early stationery featured the symbol of the arch [Osborn].

In 1938, the annual student yearbook was launched. It was named *The Arch*, after Crowell Hall's arch [De Remer, 85.] (Crowell Hall was simply called the administration building until 1945) [Gene Getz, *MBI: The Story of Moody Bible Institute* (Chicago: Moody Press, 1969), 88].

CHAPTER 16
NEWS EVENTS IN CHICAGO

Chicago has experienced many very positive events and developments. It has often been referred to as the conference center of the United States. It has much very admirable architecture and a beautiful skyline, enticing people from all over the world to come to study its architecture. It has been the home of Sears, Roebuck and Company, Montgomery Ward, Quaker Oats Company, and many other business giants. The city rebuilt admirably after the Great Chicago Fire of 1871. The city is known for great museums and exhibits, and its lively cultural attractions.

But Chicago's historical events have not always been happy ones. These are some of the negative things the city experienced during my teaching years at Moody:

On April 4, 1968, Dr. Martin Luther King was murdered in Memphis, Tennessee. Outraged, many of the residents of the west and south sides of Chicago rioted, and ten people were killed. Eight thousand regular Army and National Guard troops were placed in Chicago to quell the riots. Police squad cars with four men in each patrolled the streets of Chicago. There were brick-throwing and window-smashing. Many buildings were burned and looted. National Guard and U. S. Army trucks and jeeps were parked all over the city, including many parked on Chicago Avenue and on La Salle Street just outside Moody Bible Institute. Anticipating more trouble when Martin Luther King's funeral was held, the Moody administration dismissed classes a week early for spring break. I was saddened by the assassination and the racial tension. I was also deeply concerned for the safety of our students and Moody's campus.

While I was attending Roosevelt University in the Loop during 1968, 200 of the more radical students made strong demands for changes. Among other things, they wanted more control of the curriculum. One day there was a student strike. Another time, several Roosevelt University students were arrested for locking up the president and vice president of the university to press their demands. Keep in mind that Roosevelt was a commuter school, and I was taking only one philosophy course at a time. I tried to steer clear of the political issues, especially since my conservative perspective conflicted with that of the vast majority of Roosevelt students.

Those were the days when students throughout the country protested the Vietnam War. Students forcibly took over classrooms and administration buildings and made all sorts of demands, such as establishing courses in African American history, culture, and art, abolishing grading, having an open curriculum where students could choose anything they wanted, having free universities where courses were tuition-free and students taught courses. I felt that most of these demands were chaotic and counter-productive, but I did favor some of the curricular changes sought. Sometimes administrators or faculty members were taken hostage. The 60's was a decade of civil unrest throughout America, especially in the larger cities. The Vietnam War finally ended on January 23, 1973. America would never be the same again.

In August 1968, The National Guard was again called to Chicago to prevent rioting at the Democratic National Convention. Although our family missed the action (we drove to California on vacation), "protesters staged a demonstration against the Vietnam War in Chicago during the Democratic presidential convention. [Mayor] Daley ordered aggressive police action to quash the protest. The ensuing violence by police led to several days of rioting" ["Chicago (city, Illinois)," Microsoft Encarta '97 Encyclopedia]. Some of the battle between police and protesters took place in Lincoln Park, a mile north of Moody Bible Institute. The mounted police attempted to disperse protesters who were camping out in Lincoln Park to demonstrate the next day.

Beginning on August 23, 1972, we had the worst flooding in Illinois history, we were told. The rainfall on August 25 was 6-7 inches in a few hours! Our roof leaked a bit and the basement took in some water, but we are very fortunate to be located at the top of a hill, and that minimized the damage to our house. Many in nearby suburbs suffered severe property damage.

The worst train wreck in Chicago history occurred on October 30, 1972, when two Illinois Central commuter trains collided at the 27th Street Station. Forty-four were killed and 300 injured. I was grateful that I did not ride on that line. Later that year (December 8, 1972), a United Air Lines 737 crashed at Midway Airport, killing 45.

In October 1974, two powerful explosions were set off a few blocks from Moody, to divert attention from a $3.8 million robbery of the Perolator vault. The Perolator Company used armored trucks to transport cash to and from banks and businesses. Windows in Osborne Hall, across La Salle Street from the Torrey-Gray auditorium, were blown out by the blast. I heard the tremendous blast, but did not know at the time what had happened.

Mayor Richard J. Daley had ruled the city of Chicago as "boss" from 1955 to 1976, through five four-year terms. He had begun to serve a sixth term when, on December 20, 1976, he died of a massive heart attack at age 74. Daley was sometimes dubbed "the last of the big-city bosses" because he exerted iron-fisted control over Chicago's government and practiced widespread job patronage ["Richard Joseph Daley," *Encyclopedia* Britannica, 2001 edition].

One of our fine students, a young lady named Kristin Kent, was majoring in American Intercultural Ministries and was planning on inner city missionary service. She worked part-time as a lifeguard at the East Bank Club. As she was returning from work the night of August 4, 1984, she was attacked and murdered only a block south of Moody Bible Institute. She was the first person killed while living on campus in the nearly 100 years of MBI's history. It was a shock to the entire Moody family.

In September and October, 1986, we had two weeks of heavy rains that brought a flooding disaster to Lake, Mc Henry, and Kane counties due to the overflowing of the Des Plaines and other rivers. Some houses in Mt. Prospect were inundated with twelve feet of water!

On August 13 and 14, 1987, the Chicago area had "the flood of the century," a record 9.2 inches of rain in 24 hours. Driving was difficult in some areas. Governor Thompson declared Northern Cook and DuPage Counties disaster areas. On November 25, 1987, Mayor Harold Washington, the first African American mayor of Chicago died suddenly from a heart attack.

Every summer Chicago puts on a major recreational celebration in Grant Park, called "Taste of Chicago." Our family attended for a day in July 1990. My diary description follows: "The crowds [in Grant Park] are the largest I'd ever expect to see outside of Mecca! There were wall-to-wall people everywhere. Everyone was cordial during the day, but as the evening ground on, and they kept drinking beer, some people got pretty nasty and rowdy. This afternoon, we attended a tiny, one-ring free circus. It was really good! They had a tightrope walker, trained ponies, a dressage horse, a baby elephant, clowns, jugglers, and high-wire trapeze acts. The fireworks [in the evening] were really the best I've seen. Drunken people and kids were shooting off bottle rockets into the lake, sometimes into the boats floating around in the marina. One [boat owner] got very angry and came on shore, trying to find out who had done it. After the fireworks, we all walked back to the Chicago Northwestern Station. There was an enormous crowd of half-drunk and fully drunk young adults and teens. It was the wildest train ride I'd ever experienced. One vestibule window was broken and some near-fights happened. An irate passenger threw off several drunks at Elmhurst. So much for Taste of Chicago. Once per lifetime is enough."

Chicago suffered a disaster in the Loop (the downtown business area) in April 1992. One of the old coal tunnels near the Kinzie Street bridge was flooded by water from the Chicago River, and from there the water spread to many business buildings, flooding their basements and doing millions of dollars worth of damage.

March 1993 saw a tragic fire at the old Paxton Hotel in the 1400 block of North La Salle Blvd. that killed 17 residents.

CHAPTER 17
A CAREER ENDS

On August 30, 1994, shortly after beginning my last year of teaching at Moody, I wrote my letter of retirement and shed a few tears. The Lord had given me a wonderful ministry of 32 years at MBI, and I was sad to see it coming to an end. In April 1995, I was shocked to realize that I would never need another monthly-unlimited ticket to commute to Chicago by train!

During my last semester of teaching, in April 1995, I sensed that the Moody students were experiencing a special refreshment from the Lord. It was triggered by reports of revival among the students of Wheaton College. In response, our students began to give testimony, sing, pray, and confess their sins. On one night, a student-led meeting continued until 3 a.m.!

In my last faculty meeting of about 650 in 32 years, the Undergraduate Bylaws, on which my committee and I had worked for four years, were accepted unanimously after two slight amendments. This was on May 3, 1995. I was thrilled and relieved to successfully complete this project! (In a jocular mood, the administration threatened that I could not retire until the Bylaws were completed!) In this faculty meeting, it was announced that three of our faculty members, Leslie Keylock, Julia Graddy, and Rosalie de Rosset, had just earned their doctoral degrees.

On May 5, 1995, I was urged to attend the chapel where the student yearbook, *The Arch*, was dedicated. I was really shocked when *The Arch* for 1995 was dedicated to me! My wife, Carol, had known about it for three weeks, and was present at the chapel, along with our son, Timothy.

On May 8, 1995, I attended my retirement luncheon at Moody. The room was packed, and the luncheon and program went superbly well! Our daughters, Ruth and Joy, put on a hilarious skit about my hats for every temperature! (I nearly always wear a hat, and I have some thirty hats and baseball caps representing various schools, organizations, and foreign countries.) Carol gave a little talk, then a former student, Roger Bacon, spoke, and finally a faculty colleague, Dr. Harold Foos. An outstanding student of mine, Cristian Barbosu, was photographer. The menu was just as I requested, and delicious. It was also at this celebration that Dr. Stowell met Joy's boyfriend (not yet fiancé), Knute Axelson. Dr. Stowell, not knowing he was speaking prophetically, asked Knute, "So, how does it feel knowing that you'll have a theology professor for a father-in-law?"

The luncheon lasted about two hours. I was both happy and sad at the same time. Happy to complete a wonderful teaching career at Moody, and yet sad because my life would never be the same again. I knew that I would lose frequent contact with many of my friends, and so it has turned out.

May 13, 1995, was a very busy day for Carol and me. First, we attended my last student graduation exercises as a Moody faculty member. Greg Waybright, a former Moody student and president-elect of Trinity International University, gave the address. The same day, Carol and I went to the graduation exercises at Northern Illinois University, De Kalb, Illinois. There, we witnessed the graduation of Serge Bernard, a French student who had lived with us for six years. Finally, we drove down to Urbana, Illinois, and had dinner with our daughter Joy, on the evening before her graduation from the University of Illinois. The commencement the next day was awesome, as it was held in the big dome with lots of dignity, color, and music. Joy graduated with highest honors in her French major, and received several awards. She did well!

I felt an imposing sadness in mid-July when I crated my personal library of some 4,000 books to store until my library/office could be built at home! My books were dear friends, and I was depressed to realize that they would be unavailable for a year or so. I consoled myself at the thought that the books would be resurrected. (We had to have a 15 by 20 foot room added on to our house for my books and desk. I made the ten white pine bookshelves to hold my rather large library. Each unit was 9 feet 4 inches tall and had eight or nine shelves.) Larry Davidheiser, assistant to the academic dean, very graciously allowed me to store my seventy cartons of books in an empty Fitzwater Hall office for a whole year!

I was officially retired on July 31, 1995, the same day as our thirtieth wedding anniversary!

Bernard De Remer wrote in 1960 that Moody's arch was the gateway "through which students enter for training and depart for service." That pretty much sums up the main purpose for Moody Bible Institute. This was just as true during the 32 years I taught at Moody. By God's grace, may it ever be so in the future!

In Moody Bible Institute's early days, James M. Gray, dean, penned the words of what became known as *The Fellowship Song.* Daniel B. Towner of Moody's music faculty wrote the music. The song's second stanza goes like this:

"By blood redeemed, and heirs of God's salvation,
   Called by His Son to toil in every nation,
Far in the harvest field reaping we may wander,
   Laden with the golden grain we'll meet in glory yonder!

This stanza neatly underscores the worldwide missionary emphasis of Moody, which is still true today. "God bless the school that D. L. Moody founded"! [Opening words of *The Fellowship Song]*

Printed in the United States
48088LVS00004B/235-246